Faithfully
CHARLESTON

ST. MICHAEL'S CELEBRATES
250 YEARS OF MEALS
AND MEMORIES

ISBN 0-9709550-0-6

First Edition

First Printing   September 2001   7,500 copies
Second Printing   December 2003   10,000 copies

To order additional copies of Faithfully Charleston,
please use the order form provided in the back of the book or write:

St. Michael's Episcopal Church
14 St. Michael's Alley
Charleston, SC 29401

WIMMER
COOKBOOKS

ConsolidatedGraphics

1-800-548-2537

Table of Contents

Recipes for Relationships
Thanksgiving
About the Artist
From the Cookbook Committee
About St. Michael's Church
Contributors

Recipes for Relationships

What does a cookbook full of recipes have to do with the God-given mission of a church? More than you might imagine! The answer has to do with the development of Christian community.

One of the most important expressions used by the writers of the New Testament is the phrase, "love one another." In John 15:12, Jesus said, "This is my commandment, that you love one another, as I have loved you." St. Paul, in Romans 13:8, said, "Owe no one anything, except to love one another." And St. John, in 1 John 4:12, said, "If we love one another, God abides in us." All this talk about loving one another reminds us that the Christian life is not a private project. Anyone who truly believes in Jesus Christ will inevitably be drawn into regular contact with other believers. And from the earliest days of the Church, followers of Christ have been sharing meals with one another. While Jesus established the Lord's Supper, or Holy Communion, as the center of the church's common life, his followers also came together for fellowship meals, sometimes enjoying those gatherings so much that the apostles had to recommend rules of conduct. (1 Cor. 11:20-21) Eating together remains a vital ingredient in the life of any family, whether the family is parents and children around the dinner table or a congregation of Christian sisters and brothers at long tables in the parish hall. When the members of a family get so busy that they rarely eat together, they're likely to have a hard time maintaining love for one another. Good meals are an incentive to good family gatherings, where people can grow in love.

That's why I believe St. Michael's cookbook, *Faithfully Charleston*, will make an important contribution to the congregation's mission of building Christian community and strengthening families. These are recipes for relationships! Some of these recipes will be used for congregational dinners where long-time church members and parish newcomers can become friends. More often, in kitchens where this cookbook is used, meal planners in search of a menu that will delight the family will leaf through the recipes, admiring the illustrations of the church and remembering God's gracious provision of food to sustain life and of people to make life rich. It's in life together that we discover and learn to share the love of Christ. Thanks be to God, who so desires his people to love one another that he will bless and use for his glory cathedrals and choirs — and cookbooks!

Richard I.H. Belser

Rector

Thanksgivings

Our Heavenly Father, we thank you for the food before us, the roof above us and for this family. Help us to remember that a family is for growing up in, for going away from, and for coming back to. It is for loving concern, for helping each other through happy times and sad. With Your blessing, this family will always be together in our hearts and in our memories, giving us strength to live and to be our own person. Amen

(Parishioner Mikell Scarborough contributed this thanksgiving which was penned by his friend Robert A. Watson while a seminary student at Yale. Mr. Watson touched Mikell's soul as well as many others.)

The eyes of all wait upon you, O Lord, and you give them their food in due season. You open wide your hand, and satisfy the needs of every living creature. Give us grateful hearts, our Father, for all your mercies and make us mindful of the needs of others; through Jesus Christ our Lord. Amen.

Blessed are you, O Lord God, King of the Universe, for You give us food to sustain our lives and make our hearts glad; through Jesus Christ our Lord. Amen

Thanks be to Thee, my Lord Jesus Christ, for all the benefits and blessings which Thou has given me. O most merciful Redeemer, Friend, Brother, may I see Thee more clearly, love Thee more dearly, and follow Thee more nearly, day by day. Amen

About the Artist

William Jameson is a nationally renowned artist residing in Mt. Pleasant, SC, with his wife Anne. Both William and Anne are members of St. Michael's Church.

Mr. Jameson studied at Ringling School of Art in Sarasota, Florida and attended the Instituto Allende in San Miguel de Allende, Mexico for graduate studies. He has been a professional artist for thirty- one years with painting exhibitions from Italy to New York, the Carolinas to Texas. Jameson has taught painting on the college level and has taught privately in his studio for many years. Since 1988, he has been teaching painting workshops in the southeastern United States and in 1997 he expanded the workshop venues to Mexico, France and Italy. The "Art in Tuscany" workshop was featured in Industry Week Magazine in June of 1999.

Mr. Jameson paints daily in his studio at home - working on his favorite subjects which include the dark streams and creeks of the Carolina Piedmont and Appalachia, the harbors, creeks and rivers of the Carolina Low Country and the landscapes of Tuscany and Provence.

"Faithfully Charleston" is Mr. Jameson's third cookbook. You can visit his web site at www.williamjameson.com to view other highlighted works.

From The Cookbook Committee

Faithfully Charleston is a marvelous collection of recipes from the St. Michael's congregation. We thank everyone who shared their recipes and especially those who spent long hours and used countless ingredients testing recipes, to those who hosted testing parties, worked to raise funds, donated time and talent to our fall bazaar, contributed stories, legends, and/or recipes, and to everyone who has worked tirelessly to make "Faithfully Charleston" the beautiful book that it is today. We would also like to thank those who donated their time, treasure, and talents to make this cookbook happen.

Special thanks to:
William Jameson,
Leonard Stevens of Ambassador Graphics.

Committee Members

Beverly Howell - Chair

Janet Baker - Co-Chair

Ruthie Smythe - Marketing Chair

Ken Coker - Treasurer/Marketing Co-Chair

Kate Barnett - Testing Chair

Anne Jameson - Testing Co-Chair

Gina Hull - Design Chair

Kit Coker- Design Co-Chair

William Jameson - Artist

Frances Bramlett - Writer

Harriott Johnson - Writer

Many thanks to everyone who participated in putting this cookbook together:

Laura Lee Kinney, Mary Gladys Cummins, Harriott Johnson, Caroline Moore, Ellen Finkbine, Jane Potts, Louise Irvin, Evie Radcliffe, Betsy Reynolds.

In Loving Memory of our
friend and committee member
~ Sally Warfuel ~
whose dedication to her faith and
to St. Michael's Church is an
inspiration to all.

About St. Michael's

St. Michael's Church is the oldest church edifice in the City of Charleston, standing on the site of the first Anglican Church built south of Virginia. In the 1680's a small wooden church, the first in the new town of Charles Town, was built on this spot for the families of the Church of England, and named St. Philip's. By 1727 the town had grown too large for the small church and a more spacious one was built of brick on Church Street, later destroyed by fire in 1835.

By 1751, St. Philip's had again proved too small for the increasing population and another church was authorized by the General Assembly of the Province, to be built on the old site and to be known as St. Michael's. The cornerstone was laid in 1752 and in 1761 the church was opened for services. Except for the addition of the sacristy in 1883, on the south-east corner, the structure of the building has been little changed.

The large, long double-pew in the center of the church, No. 43, originally known as "The Governor's Pew", is the one in which President George Washington worshipped on Sunday afternoon, May 8, 1791. General Robert E. Lee also worshipped in this pew some seventy years later. The pews, native cedar, are very much the same as they have always been. The pulpit is the original one, remarkable for its height and the massive sounding board supported by two Corinthian columns. Its prominence bears out the fact that at the time the church was built, the center of interest in the service was the sermon, conflicting with the central place planned for the altar.

The present chancel decoration was executed by Tiffany in 1905. The chancel window, installed as a memorial in 1893, shows St. Michael Casting out the Dragon, after Raphael's painting. The two stained-glass windows in the north aisle, Easter Morning and The Annunciation were presented to the church in 1897 and 1908, respectively.

The clock and ring of eight bells were imported from England in 1764 and are housed in the church steeple - at a height of 186 feet. The weather-vane atop the steeple towers another 7½ feet above Charleston. During the American Revolution, the steeple was painted black supposedly to disguise it. The steeple's arcade level served as an observation post in both the Revolutionary War and the War Between the States. During this war, the bells were sent to Columbia for protection, but were burned in the great fire there. The metal was salvaged, sent to England and recast by the original founders in the original molds. After the destruction of Hurricane Hugo in 1989, the bells were again sent to England for repair and in 1993, the bells were refurbished and re-hung by Whitechapel, the original founders.

(continued on next page)

Today, the bells at St. Michael's ring out each Sunday morning welcoming one and all. Over the years, our congregation has shared joyous memories of worship, fellowship and fun - many times including food in our activities. Our Lenten Lunches, Alpha dinners, Michaelmas Sunday, Shrove Tuesday Pancake Supper, and the Brothers of St. Andrews Oyster Roast are "must attend" events where everyone enjoys food, fellowship and fun.

Charleston is steeped in tradition - and as Southerners, we are very proud to share our heritage with people all over the world. Southern hospitality is our mascot, our cornerstone - and when we say "y'all come to see us", we really mean it. When you do visit us, we hope that you will carry with you memories of magnolia blossoms, flowering azaleas and wisteria, and the sweet, sweet smell of the gardenias and honeysuckle. As you walk our beautiful streets, you may also be lucky enough to get a whiff of something delicious cooking in a Charleston kitchen. It is our hope that you will join us on this journey through Southern cooking and experience the tradition and heritage of 250 years of meals and memories.

Contributors

Bitsy Aimar

Juliana Marjenhoff Akers

Helen Allen

Janet Baker

Robert Barker

Kate Barnett

Georgianne Batts

Jan Beebe

Anne Holcomb Belser

Irvine F. Belser, Jr.

Rev. Richard I. H. Belser

John H. Bennett, Jr.

Randolph Waring Berretta

Rebecca Blanton

Sharon Baxley

Frances W. Bramlett

Susan Brandt

Kelly Brinson

Todd Brown

Peggy Buchanan

Brenda S. Burch

Nancy Butler

Sandra M. Caldwell

Marge Cappuccio

Vicki Hewitt Causey

Elizabeth Cockrell Clark

Kit Coker

Patty Cole

Anne Frizelle Coleman

Debby Walker Coleman

Heather Coleman

Libby Conway

Patrick Conway

Reverend Kris Coppinger

Jean Corbett

Johnnie Corbett

Cynthia Simmons Corley

Dr. Charles Edward Corley III

Mrs. Charles Edward Corley III

James H. Cummins, III

Rhett Crisler

Patti Daniels

Dan Davis

Mrs. C. Stuart Dawson, Jr.

Thomas Heyward Dowdney

Margaret Eastman

Dick Eichhorn

Wendy Fernau

Ellen Finkbine

Caroline de Vlaming

Marion Fletcher

Amy Fraser

Randy Gobel

Ginny Gordon

Vista Anne Grayson

Frances E. Grimball

Cindy Groseclose

Ellen W. Hamrick

Connie Hare

Kathy Hare

Sarah Hare

Beth Webb Hart

Edward Hart

Debbie Herrman

Susan Herrmann

Ashley Hewitt

Hazel Heyward

Lea Hicks

Cynthia Booth Hines

Holy Apostles Episcopal
    Church N.Y.C.

Lee Sabatino Horton

Beverly Howell

Virginia Zemp Howell

Saida Huey

Betty Hughes

Gina W. Hull

Michael Hull

Molly Hull

Mrs. James Addison Ingle

Ann Limehouse Irvin

Louise Irvin

Anne Jameson

Wendy Jimenez

Eugenia M. Johnson

Harriott Johnson

Marguerite Kennedy

Laura Lee Kinney

Merrilee Kinney

Trish Kirkland

Lynn Kornya

Noel Kunes

Hugh C. Lane, Jr.

Mary Larsen

Liz Lipscomb

Eunice Logan

Christine MacPherson

Sandy MacPherson

Karen Marjenhoff

Katherine Marjenhoff

CAPT August J. Marjenhoff, USNR (RET)

Jessica Marshall

Virginia Matthews

Frank M. McClain

Mary Lee McClain

Eliza T. McClintock

Gwen McCurdy

Trish McGuinn

Patricia McVay

Beryl Middleton

Christine Meredith

Martha Mood

Caroline H. Moore

Eleanor Moore

Kathy Moore

Emily Morrison

Mindy Mount

Cora Mueller

Patricia Murton

Ella Heyward Palmer

Mary Palmer

Tom Palmer

Cosy Pelzer

Jo Plaehn

Jane Potts

Evie Radcliffe

Emerson Read

Marie Watson Read

Betsy Reynolds

Elizabeth Riggs

Charlotte Riley

Margaret Rivers

Dot Rogers

B. J. Rumble

Tonnie Page Rushing

Caroline Russell

Mary Lemacks Scarborough

Ross Scarborough

Jane Thornhill Schachte

Charles Scherer

David Schindler

Hallie Seibels

Irene Simmons

Jo Simonds

Etta Ray Simons

Sally Smith

Cate Smythe

Cord Smythe

David Smythe

Ruthie Smythe

Susan Smythe

Tigger Smythe

Jan Snook

Elizabeth Sosnowski

Patti Sosnowski

Mary Ann Spivey

Drs. Carl and Debbie Stanitski

Sarah R. S. Stender

Sallie Storen

Cynthia Straney

Mary T. Stuckey

Elizabeth C. Tate

Margaret B. Tenney

Louise Thompson

Jane L. Thornhill

Laurie Thornhill

Mary Frances Thornhill

Winston Thornhill

Frances Tindall

Scrap Tindall

Hannah Jameson Tipper

Jenny Traslavina

Chris Turner

Lib Van Every

John Wade

Elizabeth Walker

Linda Wall

Susan Taylor Wall

Sally Warfuel

Danelle Hare Warner

Nancy Warren

Julie Waugh

Tracy Weaver

Elizabeth Williams

Boo Wilson

Margaret Wilson

Dr. William C. Wilson

Elizabeth Wood

Elizabeth J. Young

Elizabeth Zadig

Lois Dewitt Zemp

Many thanks to all who contributed recipes to *Faithfully Charleston*. Please know that every effort has been made to include each contributor's name. If you see that a name is missing, let us know so that we can gratefully include it in our next printing.

Appetizers

"In the beginning..."

Baptismal Font

Baptism by water symbolizes the washing away of our sins, marking the beginning of our journey of a life with Christ. In water Jesus received baptism by John and was anointed by the Holy Spirit as Messiah to lead us from the bondage of sin to everlasting life. The newly baptized are welcomed into the fold with the following proclamation from The Book of Common Prayer: "We receive you into the household of God. Confess the faith of Christ crucified, proclaim his resurrection and share with us in his eternal priesthood."

"And John said, 'I saw the Spirit descending from Heaven like a dove, and it remained on him. I myself did not know him, but the one who sent me to baptize with water said to me, "He on whom you see the Spirit descend and remain is the one who baptizes with the Holy Spirit." And I myself have seen and have testified that this is the Son of God.'"
John 1:32-34

Onion Pie

1 part shredded Jarlsberg cheese	1 part mayonnaise (do not use low fat)
1 part grated Vidalia onion, or other sweet onion	

Preheat oven to 350 degrees.

Combine all ingredients until mixed well. Transfer to a shallow quiche plate or baking dish. Bake, uncovered, for 30 minutes or until browned on top. Serve immediately.

He who works his land will have abundant food, but he who chases fantasies lacks judgment.

~ Proverbs 12:11

Salmon Mousse

Mousse

2 envelopes unflavored gelatin	1 cup chopped celery
½ cup cold water	1 bell pepper, chopped
1 cup mayonnaise	1 teaspoon chopped onion
⅓ cup lemon juice	2 eggs, separated
1 (16-ounce) can salmon, drained, boned and flaked	½ cup heavy cream, whipped
	Salt and pepper to taste

Sauce

Several bunches fresh dill, chopped	1 cup mayonnaise
1 cup plain yogurt	1 cup sour cream

Combine gelatin and cold water in a saucepan and let stand 1 minute. Stir over medium heat until gelatin dissolves. Cool.

Mix mayonnaise and lemon juice until smooth. Slowly blend in gelatin mixture. Chill until mixture starts to gel slightly. Fold in salmon, celery, bell pepper and onion.

Fold egg yolks into mixture. Beat egg whites until stiff and fold into mousse. Fold in whipped cream. Season with salt and pepper. Transfer to a 1-quart fish mold and refrigerate overnight. Unmold before serving.

To make sauce, combine all ingredients and chill overnight. Serve with mousse.

40 servings at a cocktail party

For a dramatic presentation at a cocktail party, decorate salmon mousse with vegetables and flowers.

Mousse Diane (Pâté)

2	(10½-ounce) cans jellied consommé, chilled		Dash of sage
			Dash of cayenne pepper
1	(8-ounce) plus 1 (3-ounce) package cream cheese	1	teaspoon lemon juice
		1	teaspoon sherry
			Chopped celery (optional)
	Dash of thyme		Chopped carrot (optional)

Combine all ingredients in a blender. Process until smooth.

Pour into small, individual-size ramekins. Decorate with caviar, sieved eggs, sliced black olives or halved lemon slices.

Serve as a first course with small slices of dark bread or put in a large dish and serve as a cocktail spread.

Smoked Oyster Spread

2	(3¾-ounce) cans petite smoked oysters, drained	1	tablespoon lemon juice
		⅛	teaspoon salt
		¼	teaspoon garlic salt
2	(8-ounce) packages cream cheese	2-3	green onions, chopped
2	teaspoons Worcestershire sauce		Dash of Tabasco sauce (optional)
			Parsley for garnish
2	tablespoons mayonnaise		

Chop drained oysters by hand. Combine oysters with remaining ingredients except parsley. Spoon into a 4-cup mold or a bowl. Chill 2 to 3 hours.

When ready to serve, unmold if in a mold. Garnish with parsley and serve with crackers.

Florence Culpepper's Shrimp Mold

2   envelopes unflavored gelatin
½   cup cold water
1   (10¾-ounce) can tomato soup, undiluted
1   (8-ounce) package cream cheese, softened
1   pound cooked and peeled shrimp, chopped
1   cup mayonnaise
½   cup finely chopped celery
¼   cup finely chopped green onion
¼   cup chopped bell pepper
¼   cup finely chopped dill and sweet pickles
5   stuffed olives, chopped
1   teaspoon salt
     Dash of cayenne pepper, or to taste
2   dashes Worcestershire sauce
2   teaspoons Tabasco sauce

Dissolve gelatin in cold water. Heat soup to a boil. Remove soup from heat and stir in gelatin. Cream cream cheese with a fork and add to soup mixture. Blend thoroughly with an electric mixer. Cool.

Add shrimp, mayonnaise, celery, green onion, bell pepper, pickles and olives. Mix well. Season with salt, cayenne pepper, Worcestershire sauce and Tabasco sauce. Adjust seasonings as needed.

Pour mixture into a well-greased 5-cup mold. Refrigerate until set, or preferably overnight. Unmold and serve with crackers.

The large square pew on the north side of the middle aisle, No. 43, is known as the Governor's Pew. On the afternoon of Sunday, May 8, 1791, George Washington worshipped in this pew, as well as Robert E. Lee seventy years later.

Deltaville Shrimp Dip or Spread

1   (8-ounce) package cream cheese
1   (8-ounce) can crushed pineapple, well drained
     Chopped green bell pepper
     Chopped onion
     Seasoning salt to taste
¾   cup cooked and chopped shrimp

Combine all ingredients and mix well. Make ahead to allow flavors to meld. Serve over crackers.

Crab Spread

1 (8-ounce) package cream cheese, softened	1 teaspoon Worcestershire sauce
½ cup mayonnaise	1 (6-ounce) can crabmeat, drained
2 ounces Cheddar cheese, grated	Black pepper to taste
Juice of 1 pressed garlic clove	Lemon juice to taste
	Parsley for garnish

Combine all ingredients except parsley. Garnish with parsley and serve with crackers or Melba toast.

Island Crab Dip

1 (8-ounce) package cream cheese	¼ teaspoon salt
1 (8-ounce) container sour cream	⅛ teaspoon coarsely ground black pepper
¼ cup mayonnaise	½ cup grated Cheddar cheese
1 tablespoon Worcestershire sauce	1 pound fresh lump crabmeat
½ teaspoon fresh lemon juice	2 tablespoons cream sherry
1 teaspoon dry mustard	Cream or milk
¼ teaspoon garlic powder	

Combine cream cheese, sour cream, mayonnaise, Worcestershire sauce, lemon juice, mustard, garlic powder, salt, pepper, and Cheddar cheese in a double boiler. Slowly heat mixture, stirring while heating.

When hot, add crabmeat and sherry. Add cream to reach desired consistency. Serve in a silver chafing dish with bland crackers.

Pickled Shrimp

4	pounds cooked shrimp	4	bay leaves, crushed
3-4	medium onions, thinly sliced	1	tablespoon horseradish
3-4	lemons, thinly sliced	1	tablespoon Worcestershire sauce
1	(3-ounce) jar capers	2	tablespoons sugar
2	(16-ounce) bottles Italian dressing		Tabasco sauce to taste
½	cup white vinegar		Salt to taste

Layer shrimp, onions, lemon slices and capers, repeating layers until all ingredients are used.

Combine dressing, vinegar, bay leaves, horseradish, Worcestershire sauce, sugar, Tabasco sauce and salt. Pour over layers. Cover and refrigerate 24 hours before serving.

12 to 15 servings

Salmon Log

1	(16-ounce) can salmon (2 cups), drained and broken up	2	teaspoons grated onion
		1	teaspoon horseradish
1	(8-ounce) package cream cheese, softened	¼	teaspoon salt
		½	teaspoon liquid smoke
		½	cup chopped pecans
1	tablespoon lemon juice	3	tablespoons chopped parsley

Combine salmon, cream cheese, lemon juice, onion, horseradish, salt, and liquid smoke. Mix well. Chill for several hours.

Shape mixture into an 8x2-inch log. Roll in pecans and parsley.

Original American recipes emerged from foods in the colonies, such as cured ham, baked sweet potatoes, stewed crabs and ducks and pickled shrimp.

Appetizers

15

Old Trawlers Crab Dip

1¼ cups mayonnaise	½ cup finely grated Cheddar cheese
1 cup white or claw crabmeat	1 teaspoon horseradish
	¼ cup French dressing

Comine all ingredients. Serve with Captain's wafers or Bremner wafers.

6 servings

For variety, add chopped green onions, garlic powder and Worcestershire sauce.

Crab and Artichoke Appetizer

1 (14-ounce) can artichoke hearts, drained and chopped	2 (6-ounce) cans crabmeat, drained
	1 cup Parmesan cheese
	1 cup mayonnaise

Combine all ingredients and transfer to a greased casserole dish. Broil until lightly browned. Serve with your favorite wheat wafer crackers.

Johnny's Pawleys Island Crab Balls

1	cup crabmeat	1	tablespoon Worcestershire sauce or to taste
1	cup crushed round butter crackers		
1	egg	1	teaspoon paprika or to taste
1	heaping teaspoon lemon juice		
1	heaping teaspoon dry mustard	4	dashes Tabasco sauce or to taste

Preheat oven to 400 degrees.

Combine all ingredients thoroughly. Form into balls and place on a baking sheet. Bake 30 minutes.

Great as crab cakes, too.

Henry Clay and Daniel Webster have worshipped in our old church.

Appetizers

Seafood Appetizer

Charlestonians may not believe it, but the "canned" seafood is quite good in this.

1	tablespoon ketchup		Juice of 1 lemon
1	teaspoon Worcestershire sauce	1	avocado, diced
1	tablespoon horseradish	2	(6-ounce) cans seafood (shrimp, clams or other), drained
1	tablespoon chopped green onion, green part only		Lettuce (optional)
	Dash of salt		Olives (optional)

Combine ketchup, Worcestershire sauce, horseradish, green onion, salt and lemon juice several hours before serving. Refrigerate to chill.

Just before serving, stir in avocado and seafood. Serve in scallop shells on a bed of lettuce. Top each with half an olive.

Seafood Dip

My husband has his own shrimp trawler, so we always use fresh shrimp and crab for this dip.

1	pound cooked shrimp, peeled
4	ounces smoked salmon
1	(8-ounce) container sour cream
1	(8-ounce) package cream cheese
1-2	tablespoons Texas Pete

Black pepper to taste
Celery salt to taste
Horseradish sauce (optional)
1 (6½-ounce) can minced clams, drained
¼ cup crabmeat

Chop shrimp in a food processor. Transfer to a bowl and set aside. Add salmon to food processor and chop. Set aside.

In a large bowl, combine sour cream and cream cheese. Add Texas Pete, pepper, celery salt and horseradish sauce. Stir in shrimp, salmon, clams and crabmeat. Mix thoroughly. If dip is too thick, add a small amount of clam juice from the can until desired consistency is reached. Refrigerate up to 48 hours. Serve with crackers or toasted bread.

Oyster Doo Dads

Great at Thanksgiving or Christmas

1 (12-count) package brown and serve finger rolls
Fresh or canned oysters
Butter

Garlic salt
Cayenne pepper
Lean thick-sliced bacon, cut into 1½-inch squares

Preheat oven to 375 degrees.

Cut rolls into four or five 1½-inch pieces. Create a pocket by removing bread in top center of each section, leaving ends intact. Discard removed portion. Place ½ to 1 oyster, depending on size, in each pocket. Top oyster with a pat of butter and sprinkle with garlic salt and cayenne pepper. Add a piece of bacon.

Place doo dads on a baking sheet. Bake 25 minutes or until rolls brown. Serve hot.

Homemade Pimento Cheese

½ (8-ounce) package cream or Neufchatel cheese (not fat free)
8 ounces Cheddar cheese, grated
2-3 tablespoons mayonnaise or as needed
2 tablespoons chopped chives or green onions
⅓ cup sliced stuffed green olives
½ cup chopped pecans
Grated Parmesan cheese

Mash cream cheese into Cheddar cheese with a fork. Mix in mayonnaise, adding desired amount to reach an easily spread consistency. Stir in chives, olives and pecans. Add Parmesan cheese as desired; spread should have a cheesy taste. Store in refrigerator. Remove from refrigerator 10 to 20 minutes before serving to allow cheese to soften for spreading.

10 to 12 servings

Luscious Pimento Cheese

"Great on sandwiches or on crackers!"

1½ pounds extra sharp white Cheddar cheese, grated
1 (10-ounce) jar stuffed green olives, drained and chopped
1 (12-ounce) jar roasted red peppers, drained and chopped
½ cup freshly grated Parmesan cheese
½ cup mayonnaise
2 tablespoons chopped parsley
½ teaspoon freshly ground black pepper
¼ teaspoon cayenne pepper
1 tablespoon minced onion
½ cup sliced almonds, toasted

Combine all ingredients. Refrigerate several hours before serving.

This was a
family recipe
of Mrs. Don
Richardson from
Georgetown, SC.
Mrs. Richardson
was the
chairman of
the cookbook
committee
that published
"Carolina Low
Country" in 1947
to benefit Prince
George's Parish
Church.

Cheese Loaf

*"Serve with cocktails or divide into
small containers for Christmas gifts."*

2	envelopes unflavored gelatin	1	small onion, finely chopped
¼	cup cold water	1	small green bell pepper, finely chopped
8	ounces sharp Cheddar cheese, grated	1	cup sliced almonds
1	(5-ounce) jar stuffed green olives, drained and sliced	1	(8-ounce) bottle Thousand Island dressing

Dissolve gelatin in cold water. Combine cheese, olives, onion and bell pepper. Add gelatin, almonds and dressing. Mix thoroughly and transfer to a crock or mold.

Chill several hours or until mixture is set. Serve with your favorite crackers. Mixture will keep up to two weeks in refrigerator.

25 servings

Brie Bowl

1	round European bread (not sourdough or pumpernickel) Melted garlic butter	1	wedge Brie cheese, rind removed
		1	French baguette, sliced Fruit such as apple and pear slices and grapes

Preheat oven to 350 degrees.

Slice off top of round bread. Scoop out inside, leaving sides intact to make a bowl. Brush lid and inside of bowl with garlic butter.

Cut Brie into chunks and place in bread bowl. Put lid on bowl and place on a baking sheet. Bake 25 minutes or until Brie melts.

Brush baguette slices with garlic butter and bake 10 minutes. Serve cheese bowl with toasted bread slices and fruit.

Cheddar Fondue Appetizer Cubes

1	large loaf French bread, 1 to 2 days old	8	ounces sharp Cheddar cheese, grated
½	cup butter	¼	teaspoon garlic powder
1	(8-ounce) package cream cheese	2	egg whites, beaten stiff

Cut untrimmed bread into ¾-inch cubes. Set aside.

Meanwhile, melt butter and cream cheese in a double boiler over gently boiling water. Gradually add Cheddar cheese and stir until melted and smooth. Stir in garlic powder.

Remove from heat and quickly fold in egg whites. Dip bread cubes in cheese mixture and set on wax paper for about 2½ hours. If desired, freeze dipped cubes until firm, then transfer to zip-top plastic bags and freeze until ready to use.

To serve, preheat oven to 350 degrees. Place desired number of dipped cubes on an ungreased baking sheet. Bake 6 to 8 minutes or until hot. If cubes are frozen, bake 10 to 12 minutes.

35 servings

If you have children or grandchildren who like to get messy and "help" with cooking, let them dip the bread into the cheese mixture. This is a helpful way to get "gooey"!

Hot Brie

¾	cup finely chopped pecans	3	tablespoons brown sugar
¼	cup coffee-flavored liqueur	1	(14-ounce) Brie cheese

Microwave pecans on high, stirring every 2 minutes, for 4 to 6 minutes or until toasted. Add liqueur and sugar. Stir well.

Remove and discard rind from top of Brie cheese. Spoon pecan mixture over top of cheese. Microwave cheese on high for 1½ to 2 minutes, turning a half turn after 1 minute, until cheese softens to desired consistency. Serve with Melba toast or crackers.

12 servings

June's Famous Cheese Ball

2	cups grated sharp Cheddar cheese	½	teaspoon Worcestershire sauce
1	(8-ounce) package cream cheese	3	tablespoons mayonnaise
	Dash of garlic salt	¼	cup chopped olives
3-5	dashes celery salt	¾	cup chopped pecans or parsley
2	tablespoons finely grated onion		

Combine all ingredients by hand except pecans or parsley. Form into a ball or log and chill for 2 hours.

Roll into chopped pecans or parsley. Serve with crackers.

12 servings

Beer Cheese Dip

1	(8-ounce) package extra sharp Cheddar cheese	¼	cup dark beer Dash of cayenne pepper, or to taste
1	(8-ounce) package cream cheese (regular or light)		

Combine cheeses in a microwave-safe bowl. Microwave on high 5 to 8 minutes or until cheese melts, stirring as needed while cooking. Stir in beer and cayenne pepper. Microwave 30 seconds or until warm. Serve immediately with tortilla chips.

8 servings

Tigger's Blue Cheese Dip

Kids love this! We use Krunchers plain potato chips.

1 **(24-ounce) container cottage cheese (regular or fat free)**	¼ **cup mayonnaise**
	2 **tablespoons milk or as needed**
8 **ounces blue cheese**	

Combine all ingredients in a food processor or mixer. Blend until smooth. Add as much milk as needed to reach desired consistency. Refrigerate until ready to serve.

Serve with very crunchy potato chips.

10 servings

Curry Cheese Spread

1 **(8-ounce) package cream cheese, softened**	½ **teaspoon curry**
	¼ **teaspoon dry mustard**
¼ **cup Major Grey's chutney, cut into small pieces**	¼ **cup chopped almonds**

Combine all ingredients. Refrigerate several hours. Serve with crackers.

4 to 6 servings

Curry cheese mixture spread on raisin bread makes a delicious appetizer or tea sandwich.

Onion and Cheese Spread

1 **pound Swiss cheese, grated**	1 **large onion, finely chopped**
1 **cup mayonnaise**	

Preheat oven to 350 degrees.

Melt cheese with mayonnaise in microwave. Stir in onion. Spoon mixture into a shallow baking dish.

Bake 30 minutes or until browned. Serve hot with party rye bread or crackers.

23

Texas Caviar

2	(16-ounce) cans black-eyed peas, drained	1	tablespoon sugar
2	green onions, chopped	1	tablespoon salt
2	tomatoes, chopped	1	tablespoon black pepper
½	large green bell pepper, chopped	1	tablespoon ground cumin
½	large red bell pepper, chopped	1	(16-ounce) jar thick and chunky salsa, mild or medium or combination
¼	cup Italian dressing		
½	cup chopped onion	½	cup chopped cilantro

Combine all ingredients except cilantro and refrigerate at least 8 hours before serving. Two hours before serving add cilantro. Adjust ingredient amounts as desired. Serve with taco chips.

Black-Eyed Susans

"Good for any occasion, formal or casual!"

1	cup butter, softened	½	teaspoon salt
1	pound sharp Cheddar cheese, grated	1	pound pitted dates, halved lengthwise
2	cups all-purpose flour		Poppy seeds
1	teaspoon cayenne pepper		

Preheat oven to 275 degrees.

Cream butter and cheese. Add flour, cayenne pepper and salt and mix until well combined. Cover with plastic and chill dough.

Divide dough in half, keeping half refrigerated while working with other half. Roll dough to ⅛-inch thickness. Cut out with a 2-inch biscuit cutter. Place a date half on each round. Fold dough over date and pinch together. Continue until all dough is used.

Sprinkle with poppy seeds and place on an ungreased baking sheet. Bake 35 to 40 minutes.

5 to 6 dozen

Edam Cheese Ball

1	(2 pound) Edam cheese ball	4	slices dried beef (in a jar)
8	ounces sour cream	¼	cup pimento, diced
2	tablespoons mayonnaise	2	green onions, finely chopped
¼	cup black olives	¼	teaspoon garlic salt

Allow cheese to stand at room temperature for several hours to soften. Cut top off cheese. Scoop out cheese, being very careful to leave the shell intact. Mix cheese with above ingredients. Place mixture into scooped-out shell and replace top. You will have some of the mixture left to refill shell. Make ahead 24 hours so that flavors have time to blend. Refrigerate.

Makes about 5 cups. Serves 30 to 40.

Hog's Head Cheese

For many years, Hog's Head Cheese was one of the most popular items sold at the St. Michael's Bazaar held in the fall. Other specialties that attracted buyers were pickles, jellies, venison pâté and shrimp paste. The special cake treat was the Lady Baltimore Cake, but the hottest item was always the Hog's Head Cheese.

Boiling a hog's head is a long and smelly process as a result very few St. Michael's ladies would make it. One of the last who did was Mrs. Katherine Ravenel.

The Bazaar would be the occasion that the ladies of St. Michael's forgot to be ladies, pushing and shoving at the door just before three o'clock to get at the hog's head cheese. When the doors did open, there would be a crushing avalanche, hands flying, grabbing at the delicacy, wrapped as a ball in wax paper. In a few minutes, all would be gone, until the next year's food sale.

Ingredients for Hog's Head Cheese

hog's head

allspice

vinegar

salt

hot pepper, catsup or hot sauce to taste

The Commisnor
of the Church Bill

February 17, 1752

A celebration was conducted at John Gordon's on February 17, 1752 following the laying of the first stone for St. Michael's Church. The following bill was presented and paid for this occasion:

Dinner	20 :	0 :	0	pounds
Tody	1 :	10 :	0	
Punch	5 :	0 :	0	
Beer	5 :	10 :	0	
Wine	5 :	5 :	0	
Glass Broak	:	5 :	0	
8 Magnum bonos of Claret	24 :	0 :	0	
Total	61 :	10 :	0	pounds

Frannie's Eggplant Caviar

AKA "Poor Man's Caviar"

2	large eggplants	4	anchovy filets, rinsed, dried and chopped, or 1 tablespoon anchovy paste
1	red onion, sliced		
3-4	large cloves garlic, minced		
½	cup olive or canola oil, or combination	¼	cup chopped fresh basil
2	cups peeled, seeded and diced Roma tomatoes, or 1 (14-ounce) can diced tomatoes	1	tablespoon chopped fresh thyme, or 1 teaspoon dried
		1	lemon, halved, divided
¼-½	teaspoon ground cumin		Kosher salt and freshly ground black pepper to taste
	Dash of cayenne pepper		Extra virgin olive oil (for finishing)

Preheat oven to 400 degrees.

Cut eggplants in half lengthwise and place, cut-side down, on a lightly greased baking sheet. Roast about 40 minutes or until soft to the touch. Remove and set aside to cool.

Meanwhile, sauté onion and garlic in olive oil for 10 minutes or until starting to soften. Add tomatoes and simmer about 15 minutes. Scoop out eggplant pulp, coarsely chop and add to tomato mixture. Cook about 10 minutes longer. Add cumin, cayenne pepper, anchovies, basil and thyme. Squeeze in juice of half the lemon. Simmer a few minutes more. Season with salt and pepper. Remove from heat and cool slightly.

Puree tomato mixture in batches in a food processor. Add juice from remaining half of lemon and stir in a little extra virgin olive oil. Refrigerate for at least 1 hour, although mixture is better on second day. Store up to 2 weeks in refrigerator. Use as a dip for crusty croutons or crudités, or as a pizza base or pasta sauce.

Aunt Jane's Hot Bean Dip

This is very easy and good!

1	(8-ounce) package cream cheese
1	(10-ounce) can bean dip
1	cup sour cream
½	cup chopped green onions

½	(1-ounce) package taco seasoning mix
	Tabasco sauce to taste (optional)
8	ounces Monterey Jack cheese, grated

Preheat oven to 350 degrees.

Combine all ingredients except grated cheese. Spread half of bean mixture in a quiche pan or shallow casserole dish. Top with half of grated cheese. Repeat layers.

Bake 20 minutes or until hot. Serve immediately with large corn chips or crackers.

Stuffed Mushrooms

16	ounces medium to large mushrooms, washed
¼	cup chopped onion
1	tablespoon chopped garlic
2½	tablespoons olive oil

¾	cup dry white wine
1¼	cups seasoned bread crumbs
½	cup water or more as needed
1	tablespoon Parmesan cheese

Preheat oven to 400 degrees.

Remove mushroom stems. Set mushroom caps aside and chop the stems. Sauté chopped stems, onion and garlic in oil. Add wine.

Place bread crumbs in a small mixing bowl. Add sautéed mixture with any juices. Add ½ cup water, using more if needed to reach desired consistency. Mix in Parmesan cheese. Fill mushroom caps with stuffing mixture and place on a lightly greased baking sheet. Bake 15 to 20 minutes.

16 servings

For variety, add crabmeat or minced clams to the stuffing mixture.

Tomato Surprise

Red, ripe tomatoes,
    sliced ¼-inch thick
Extra virgin olive oil
Salt and pepper
Minced garlic

Carr's water biscuits or
    whole-wheat crackers
Boursin or chèvre
    cheese (without
    herbs)

Preheat oven to 200 degrees.

Spread tomato slices in a single layer on a baking sheet. Drizzle slices with olive oil and season with salt and pepper. Sprinkle garlic on top.

Bake 6 hours. Spread biscuits, crackers or party bread with cheese and top with tomato.

Make delicious cucumber or tomato sandwiches using mayonnaise mixed with chopped fresh or dried dill. Serve open face.

Curry Dip

1   (8-ounce) package
    cream cheese,
    softened

⅔   cup chutney
⅛   teaspoon dry mustard
⅛   teaspoon curry

Combine all ingredients. Serve at room temperature as an appetizer.

Makes a delicious cocktail sandwich with raisin bread.

Bacon 'n Cheese Mushrooms

½   cup bread crumbs
½   cup Parmesan cheese
¼   cup grated Cheddar
    cheese
1   (12-ounce) package
    bacon, cooked crisp
    and crumbled

1   tablespoon mayonnaise
    or as needed
5   dozen large
    mushrooms, washed,
    stems discarded

Preheat oven to 350 degrees.

Mix bread crumbs and cheeses. Stir in crumbled bacon. Add mayonnaise and mix. Spoon mixture into mushroom caps and place on an ungreased baking sheet.

Bake 15 to 20 minutes or until heated through. Serve in a chafing dish.

25 to 30 servings

Pickled Mushrooms

⅔	cup tarragon vinegar		Dill seed
½	cup salad oil	2	tablespoons water
1	clove garlic, minced (optional)		Dash of Tabasco sauce
1	tablespoon sugar	1	medium onion, cut into rings
1½	teaspoons salt	2	(6-ounce) cans mushrooms, or 4 cups fresh mushrooms
	Freshly ground black pepper		

Combine vinegar, oil, garlic, sugar, salt, pepper, dill seed, water and Tabasco sauce in a bowl. Add onions and mushrooms in layers. Refrigerate at least 8 hours, stirring several times while marinating.

Broccoli Dip

Great for a party!

2	onions, chopped	1	(10¾-ounce) can cream of mushroom soup
½	cup butter		
2	cups chopped celery	1	(8-ounce) package cream cheese, softened
1	(10-ounce) package frozen chopped broccoli		
1	(6-ounce) roll garlic cheese	1	(2-ounce) package slivered almonds

Sauté onions in butter. Add celery and simmer until tender. Add broccoli, garlic cheese, soup, cream cheese and almonds. Heat thoroughly. Serve hot in a chafing dish with crackers or chips.

Fruit Salsa

½ cantaloupe, peeled and
    diced
1 (8-ounce) can crushed
    pineapple, drained
1 yellow bell pepper,
    diced

1 jalapeño pepper,
    seeded and diced
½-1 cup chopped fresh
    cilantro

Mix all ingredients together. Refrigerate 30 to 60 minutes
before serving. Serve with chips.

4 servings

*The fruit of
the righteous
is a tree of life
and he who wins
souls is wise.*

~ Proverbs 11:30

Black Bean-Mango Salsa

2 cups diced mango
    (½-inch dice)
1 (15 to 16-ounce) can
    black beans, drained
    and rinsed
¾ cup fresh white corn
    kernels
¾ cup finely chopped red
    onion

½ cup chopped fresh
    cilantro
1 teaspoon chili oil
1 teaspoon sugar
3 tablespoons fresh lime
    juice
    Salt and pepper to
    taste

Combine all ingredients. Best made the day before serving.

8 to 10 servings

C's Cilantro Salsa

¼ cup chopped fresh
    cilantro
3-4 green onions, chopped
1 (4-ounce) can chopped
    green chiles
1 (4-ounce) can sliced
    black olives

1 cup Italian salad
    dressing
4 ounces Monterey Jack
    cheese, grated
1 medium tomato, diced

Combine all ingredients in a bowl. Mix well. Serve with
tortilla chips.

Walnuts Rosemary

6	tablespoons butter	3	dashes cayenne pepper
1	tablespoon dried rosemary, crumbled	1	teaspoon salt
		4	cups walnut halves

Preheat oven to 325 degrees.

Melt butter. Add rosemary, cayenne pepper and salt to butter. Add walnuts and toss well. Spread walnuts in a single layer on a baking sheet.

Bake, shaking pan occasionally, about 12 minutes or until walnuts are richly browned. Serve while still warm or allow to cool.

16 servings

Pecans work well in this recipe, too.

Devine Date Appetizer

1	(8-ounce) package pitted dates	1	(1-pound) package bacon
1	(2-ounce) package slivered almonds		

Preheat oven to 400 degrees.

Place desired number of dates on a broiler pan. Put a few slivered almonds in each date cavity. Wrap one-fourth slice bacon around each date and secure with a toothpick.

Bake about 10 minutes or until bacon browns. Serve warm.

Dijon Bacon Dip

1	cup mayonnaise	1	tablespoon prepared horseradish
½	cup Dijon mustard		
4	strips bacon, cooked and crumbled, or ½ cup real bacon bits		

Combine all ingredients and mix well. Cover and refrigerate until serving time. Serve as a dip for pretzels or cut-up vegetables.

Merrilee's Easy Cheese Crisps

"Great on cocktail table instead of peanuts."

3 cups grated sharp Cheddar cheese	¼ teaspoon cayenne pepper
1½ cups unsalted butter, softened	3 cups flour
	3 cups crispy rice cereal

Preheat oven to 350 degrees.

Combine cheese and butter until well mixed. Combine cayenne pepper and flour and blend into cheese mixture. Mix in cereal.

Shape mixture into ¾-inch balls. Place balls on an ungreased baking sheet and flatten with a fork. Bake 10 minutes.

20 dozen

Florida Gators

1 (16-ounce) jar processed cheese spread	2 dashes Worcestershire sauce
½ cup butter, softened	Dash of Tabasco sauce
3 tablespoons frozen orange juice concentrate, thawed and undiluted	2 cups sifted all-purpose flour
	½ teaspoon cayenne pepper
1 tablespoon orange zest	1 teaspoon salt
	¾ cup finely chopped pecans

Perfect for tailgating at football games, hence the name "gators" for the University of Florida.

Preheat oven to 400 degrees.

Cream cheese spread and butter. Add orange juice, zest, Worcestershire sauce and Tabasco sauce. Sift together flour, cayenne pepper and salt. Add dry ingredients to cheese mixture. Mix well. Stir in pecans. Chill until firm, or freeze until ready to use.

Drop by teaspoonfuls onto a baking sheet. Press mounds flat with fingers or a floured glass bottom. Bake 7 to 8 minutes.

About 80

Cheese Crisps

½	cup butter	1	teaspoon salt
2	cups grated sharp Cheddar cheese		Tabasco or red pepper sauce to taste
1	cup flour		Pecan halves

Preheat oven to 350 degrees.

Blend all ingredients except pecans. Divide mixture into 2 balls. Roll each ball into a log about 1-inch in diameter. Wrap each log in wax paper and chill.

When cold, slice logs very thin and place slices on an ungreased baking sheet. Place a pecan half on top of each slice. Bake 10 to 15 minutes.

100 crisps

Caponatina

My grandmother would make this eggplant treat before many holiday meals. Her name was Vincenza Casiopo Sabatino.

1	large eggplant	2	tablespoons raisins
	Salt	1	cup tomato puree
1	cup diced celery	½	cup wine vinegar
½	cup olive oil	2	tablespoons sugar
1	large onion, chopped or thinly sliced		Salt and pepper to taste
3	tablespoons capers	2	loaves Italian bread or French baguettes, sliced
½	cup pitted green olives, sliced if large		

Peel eggplant, if desired, and dice. Sprinkle lightly with salt and place in a colander. Let stand 30 minutes to 2 hours to allow water to drain. Meanwhile, simmer celery in water 8 minutes. Drain and set aside to cool.

Sauté eggplant in oil in a skillet until lightly browned. Remove eggplant with a slotted spoon. Add onion to skillet and sauté until lightly browned. Add eggplant, celery, capers, olives, raisins and tomato puree to skillet.

Heat vinegar in a saucepan. Add sugar and stir until dissolved. Pour mixture over eggplant mixture. Season with salt and pepper. Simmer 15 to 20 minutes. Serve on bread slices.

20 to 25 servings

Spinach Balls

2 (10-ounce) packages
  frozen spinach,
  cooked and drained
2 cups packaged herb
  stuffing mix
2 medium onions,
  chopped
3 eggs, beaten
½ cup butter, melted

½ cup Parmesan cheese
½ teaspoon thyme
½ teaspoon black pepper
  Garlic powder to taste
  (optional)
  Tabasco sauce to taste
  (optional)
  Prepared horseradish to
  taste (optional)

Preheat oven to 300 degrees.

Combine all ingredients and form into small balls. Bake
20 minutes.

60 balls

Hanky Pankys

1 pound ground chuck
1 pound hot sausage
1 (1-pound) package
  processed cheese
  loaf, diced

2 teaspoons oregano
½ teaspoon garlic salt
1 tablespoon
  Worcestershire sauce
2 loaves party rye bread

Brown ground chuck and sausage. Drain fat. Add cheese,
oregano, garlic salt and Worcestershire sauce. Stir until
cheese melts slightly.

Spread on bread slices. Place on a baking sheet and freeze
until firm. Transfer to plastic zip-top bags and store in
freezer until ready to serve.

To serve, broil until cheese melts and is bubbly.

24 servings

*Do not love
sleep or you
will grow poor;
stay awake and
you will have
food to spare.*

~ Proverbs 20:13

*These are great for
fast lunches when
made on regular
size bread. Make
great appetizers on
cocktail bread.*

Appetizers

This is a time consuming recipe to prepare for a large crowd, but well worth the effort. For a shortcut, buy frozen meatballs and just make the sauce.

Any leftovers are delicious served over rice or noodles.

Swedish Meatballs

Use as an appetizer or a main dish.

Meatballs

3	pounds lean ground beef	1	(1-ounce) envelope dry onion soup mix
2	pounds ground chuck	2	eggs, slightly beaten
1	small to medium onion, chopped		Salt and pepper to taste

Sauce

6	(10¾-ounce) cans condensed cream of mushroom soup	1	(1-ounce) envelope dry onion soup mix
3	soup cans water		Salt and pepper to taste
		1	pound large mushrooms

Preheat oven to 350 degrees.

To make meatballs, combine ground meat, onion, soup mix and eggs. Season with salt and pepper. Mix thoroughly and roll into small balls. Place balls on an ungreased baking sheet. Bake 30 minutes or until done.

For sauce, combine soup, water and soup mix in a large Dutch oven. Season with salt and pepper. Simmer 20 to 30 minutes, stirring frequently.

Add cooked meatballs to sauce and simmer about 1 hour. Add mushrooms and cook 15 to 20 minutes longer, stirring frequently.

15 servings

Callie's Mexican Dip

1	pound Jimmy Dean regular sausage	1	can Rotel tomatoes
1	pound cream cheese, not lite		

Brown sausage and drain. Mix all together. Heat in shallow baking dish until slightly brown and bubbly – 30 minutes at 350 degrees. Serve warm with taco chips.

Sweet and Sour Chicken Wings

3	pounds chicken wings	½	cup sugar
1	cup cornstarch	¼	cup soy sauce
2	eggs, beaten	3	tablespoons ketchup
	Vegetable oil	2	tablespoons lemon
½	cup red currant jelly		juice
½	cup white vinegar		

Cut off and discard chicken wing tips. Cut remainder of wing in half at the joint. Dredge chicken in cornstarch, coating well. Dip in egg.

Pour oil into a Dutch oven to a depth of 2 to 3 inches. Heat oil to 375 degrees. Add chicken and fry until golden brown. Drain on paper towels. Transfer chicken in a 9x13-inch baking dish; set aside.

Preheat oven to 350 degrees.

Combine jelly, vinegar, sugar, soy sauce, ketchup and lemon juice in a small saucepan. Bring to a boil over medium heat. Reduce heat and simmer, uncovered, for 10 minutes. Pour over chicken. Bake 30 minutes, basting once.

About 3 dozen

Pisgah's Manna

I carried the manna to Sunday school in a napkin-covered basket and watched the children gobble it up along with three beautiful roast quail on a pretty blue and white platter. Ask our rector for that recipe. It should begin, "First shoot three quail..."

While teaching Sunday school to St Michael's 4 and 5 year olds, I had the help of a unique and dignified patchwork bear named "Pisgah." He was from the mountains of North Carolina.

We liked to make the Bible stories come alive in "you are there" fashion. The story of Moses was a three part epic with the Israelites' trek through the desert particularly exciting. I told Rick (Reverend Richard Belser) I'd like to produce the "quail and manna" the Lord provided to feed the people. That meant concocting manna to Biblical specifications that didn't resemble anything the children had ever seen or tasted. Rick said, "I'll produce the quail, you produce the manna."

I spent a Saturday making messes with honey, burning every batch. Finally I came up with this recipe. It is light and delicious.

2 sticks softened butter	1 loaf Pepperidge Farm
1 cup sugar	Very Thin white
Grated rind of 2 oranges	bread

Cream the butter, sugar and orange rind. Cut slices of bread into quarters, trimming crust. Spread with butter and bake on an ungreased cookie sheet at 200 to 225 degrees for one hour, until golden brown and crisp. Store in an airtight container.

Soups & Beverages

"...and they came two by two."

Door, Dog and Bike

Who are you waiting for my friend?
Or is it your turn to go in? Each year we ask God's
blessing at a special service of St. Francis of Assisi,
patron saint to the animals. One of the most cherished
children's hymns speaks volumes: "All things bright
and beautiful, all creatures great and small. All things
wise and wonderful, the Lord God made them all."

"And every beast after his kind, and all
cattle after their kind and every creeping thing that
creepeth upon the earth after his kind, and every fowl
of his kind, every bird of every sort. And they went
unto Noah into the ark, two and two of all flesh,
wherein is the breath of life."
Genesis 7:14-15

True Blue Creek House Clam Chowder

1	quart cherrystone clams (about 35)	½	(16-ounce) bottle ketchup
8	medium potatoes	¼	cup Worcestershire sauce
8	medium onions	1	tablespoon Tabasco sauce (optional)
2	(8-ounce) cans tomato paste	¼	cup bacon drippings or olive oil
2	(16-ounce) cans stewed tomatoes		Salt and pepper to taste

Wash unopened clams well to remove all grit and pluff mud. Pry open shell and scoop out clams, reserving liquid. Grind clams with potatoes and onions and place in a large pot along with reserved clam liquid. Cook 15 minutes, stirring occasionally.

Add tomato paste, tomatoes, ketchup, Worcestershire sauce, Tabasco sauce and bacon drippings. Season with salt and pepper. Bring to a boil. Reduce heat to low and cook 1½ hours. Add water if mixture becomes too thick.

About 8 cups

This recipe can be doubled and freezes beautifully.

If desired, use fresh frozen clams. Wash clams before freezing. When ready to use, place frozen clams in kitchen sink and run tepid water over them. After clams begin to open slightly, pry open and scoop out the frozen clams and liquid.

Soups & Beverages

Shrimp Bisque

1	medium to large onion, minced	2	tablespoons flour
¾	cup minced celery	1	quart 2% milk
	Butter for sautéing	¾	teaspoon salt
1	pound peeled and deveined medium shrimp	½	teaspoon Tabasco sauce
		1¼	teaspoons paprika
		2	teaspoons fresh lemon juice

Sauté onion and celery in butter until tender. Add shrimp and cook 2 minutes. Blend in flour. Gradually stir in milk. Add salt, Tabasco sauce, paprika and lemon juice. Bring to a boil. Reduce heat and simmer about 5 minutes. Serve over rice.

6 to 7 servings

Lobster and Celery Bisque

A delicate and different choice for a first course at dinner.

1	cup thinly sliced celery	1	(5-ounce) can lobster meat, or fresh lobster
½	cup chopped celery leaves	1	teaspoon salt
3	tablespoons coarsely chopped onion	½	teaspoon white pepper
¼	cup butter	½	cup light cream
¼	cup all-purpose flour	1	teaspoon lemon juice
3	cups milk		Chopped parsley for garnish
2	cups chicken broth		

Sauté celery, celery leaves and onion in butter until celery is tender. Remove from heat and blend in flour. Return to heat and cook and stir until mixture is bubbly. Stir in milk and broth. Cook and stir until sauce is slightly thickened.

Add lobster, salt, pepper and cream. Cook 2 to 3 minutes or until just hot; do not boil. Add lemon juice. Garnish individual servings with parsley.

7 servings

Oyster Stew

"The best"

¾ cup heavy cream per
person
Freshly shucked oysters
(a little or a lot - it's
up to you!)
Reserved oyster juice
Worcestershire sauce
to taste

Butter for sautéing
3 saltines, crushed, per
person
Onion salt to taste
Black pepper to taste
Inner celery stalks with
leaves, finely chopped
Butter for garnish

Heat cream in a saucepan until almost boiling; do not boil.
At the same time, combine oysters, oyster juice,
Worcestershire sauce and butter in a skillet and sauté until
edge of oysters just begin to curl.

Add oyster mixture, saltines, onion salt, pepper and celery
to hot cream. Heat over low heat until you see one bubble.
Pour into individual serving bowls. Garnish each serving
with a dab of butter in the center.

This stew is even better the next day.

Cheese Soup

½ cup chopped carrot
½ cup chopped onion
½ cup chopped celery
½ cup butter
⅓ cup flour
4 (10¾-ounce) cans
chicken broth, heated

2 cups hot milk
3 cups tightly packed
grated sharp Cheddar
cheese
Salt and pepper to taste

Sauté carrot, onion and celery in butter in a large skillet for
10 minutes or until tender. Blend in flour. Cook and stir 2
minutes. Vigorously whisk in hot broth all at once. Blend in
milk and cook and stir 2 minutes or until mixture thickens.

Stir in cheese. Reduce heat and simmer, stirring occasionally
until cheese melts. Season with salt and pepper.

Christmas Eve Oyster Bisque

Soups & Beverages

Great for Christmas Eve with country ham biscuits and fruitcake.

2	large carrots, julienned	1	large bay leaf
2	large onions, julienned		Salt and pepper to
2	large leeks, julienned		taste
6	celery stalks, julienned	4	tablespoons butter
5	tablespoons butter	32	fresh oysters, drained
¼	cup flour	2	teaspoons
6	cups hot fish and/or		Worcestershire sauce
	chicken broth, or	3	egg yolks
	combination	2	cups sour cream
2	cups dry white wine		

Sauté carrots, onions, leeks and celery in 5 tablespoons butter in a covered 3-quart saucepan for 10 to 15 minutes or until tender. Blend in flour and cook over low heat for 3 minutes. Cool 2 minutes. Blend in 2 cups of broth in a slow, steady stream. Gradually add remaining broth and wine. Add bay leaf. Simmer 10 minutes. Season with salt and pepper.

Heat 4 tablespoons butter in a skillet until bubbling. Add drained oysters and sauté until plump. Season with salt and pepper. Add Worcestershire sauce. Fold oyster mixture into broth mixture. If preparing ahead, refrigerate until ready to serve.

Just before serving, reheat soup. Remove 2 cups of hot soup and whisk with egg yolks and sour cream in a separate bowl. Stir mixture into the soup. Heat soup over medium heat until slightly thickened; do not bring to a simmer. Serve immediately.

8 servings

Oyster Gumbo

As a first course soup or certainly as a main dish

5	tablespoons butter	10	drops hot pepper sauce
2¼	cups chopped onion	1	(10-ounce) package
2	cups diagonally sliced		frozen sliced okra
	celery	1½	pints oysters,
⅓	cup flour		undrained
2	teaspoons salt	1½	tablespoons coarsely
1	quart water		chopped green onion
1	(16-ounce) can chunky	2	tablespoons chopped
	tomatoes		fresh parsley
½	teaspoon thyme	6-8	servings hot cooked rice
1	bay leaf		

Melt butter in a Dutch oven. Add onion and celery and cook until tender but not browned. Blend in flour and salt. Stir in water, tomatoes, thyme, bay leaf and pepper sauce. Bring to a boil. Reduce heat, cover and simmer 20 minutes.

Add okra and simmer, covered, 10 minutes longer or until okra is done. Add oysters with liquid. Simmer, uncovered, until edge of oysters curl. Sprinkle with green onions and parsley. Spoon mounds of cooked rice into individual serving bowls. Pour gumbo over rice and serve.

6 to 8 servings

Cream of Cauliflower Soup

1	head cauliflower, cut	3	tablespoons butter,
	into florets, or		melted
	1 (16-ounce) package	2	egg yolks
	frozen	½	cup cream
3	cups chicken broth		Salt and freshly ground
2	tablespoons flour		pepper to taste

Cook cauliflower in broth in a heavy pot until softened. Mix flour and butter until smooth. Blend mixture into broth. Bring to a boil. Process soup in a blender until smooth. Return soup to pot.

In a separate bowl, beat egg yolks and cream together and add to soup. Season soup with salt and pepper. Cook until hot; do not boil.

5 to 6 cups

Black Bean and Beef Chili

May use boneless butt or chicken.
(Reduce cooking time by half if using chicken.)

1½ cups dried black beans, or 2 (16-ounce) cans black beans
1 (3½-pound) boneless beef sirloin or beef tip
2 tablespoons olive oil
2 onions, chopped
6 cloves garlic, minced
2 tablespoons olive oil
⅓ cup mild pure chili powder
1½ tablespoons ground cumin
1½ tablespoons ground oregano
1 teaspoon cayenne pepper or to taste
2 teaspoons salt
1 (14½-ounce) can plum tomatoes, undrained
3½ cups chicken broth
   Cooked white rice
   Sour cream and cilantro for garnish

Rinse and pick through dried beans and place in a pot. Cover with water by 2 inches. Bring to a boil and cook 1 minute. Remove from heat and cover. Let stand for 1 hour. Drain and add new water. Bring to a boil. Reduce heat and simmer 45 minutes or until tender. Cool and drain. If using canned beans, drain, rinse and drain.

Trim fat from beef and cut beef into ½-inch cubes. Heat 2 tablespoons oil in a casserole dish. Add onions and garlic and cook over medium heat for 20 minutes or until onions are softened. Remove onions and garlic and set aside.

Add 2 tablespoons oil to same dish. Add beef and cook over medium heat, stirring occasionally, for 15 minutes or until meat is browned. Stir in onions and garlic, chili powder, cumin, oregano, cayenne pepper and salt. Cook and stir 5 minutes, Add undrained tomatoes and broth. Break up tomatoes and bring to a boil. Reduce heat and simmer, uncovered, for 1 hour, stirring occasionally.

Adjust seasonings to taste. Continue to simmer 50 to 60 minutes or until meat is tender and chili is thick. Stir in beans and heat thoroughly. Serve over cooked rice. Top individual servings with sour cream and cilantro.

6 to 8 servings

Artichoke Soup

1 (13¾-ounce) can artichoke hearts, drained and quartered
1 (10¾-ounce) can condensed cream of celery soup
1 (10¾-ounce) can condensed cream of chicken soup
1 soup can of whole milk
⅓ cup grated carrot
¼ cup chopped onion
½ teaspoon curry
Dash of Tabasco sauce
1 soup can of half-and-half
1 cup cooked shrimp

Combine artichoke hearts, undiluted soups, milk, carrot, onion, curry and Tabasco sauce in a saucepan. Cook over low heat for 30 minutes.

Stir in half-and-half and shrimp. Heat until warm.

Old Fashioned Squash Soup

1 medium onion, finely chopped
4 tablespoons butter
2 tablespoons flour
¾ teaspoon salt
Dash of black pepper
⅓ teaspoon ground nutmeg
1 (14-ounce) can chicken broth
1 cup milk
1½ cups cooked yellow squash
2 teaspoons Worcestershire sauce
1 egg yolk, slightly beaten
½ cup heavy cream

Sauté onion in butter over medium heat for 5 minutes or until softened. Blend in flour, salt, pepper and nutmeg. Stir until bubbly.

Remove from heat and stir in broth and milk. Add squash and Worcestershire sauce. Mix egg yolk and cream together, then add to soup. Heat until hot, do not boil. Serve immediately.

Butternut Squash Soup

1	large sweet onion, chopped	1	large butternut squash, peeled and diced
1	leek, chopped	1	quart chicken broth
2	stalks celery, peeled and chopped	1	cup heavy cream
3	strips smoked bacon (optional)	2	tablespoons honey
			Salt and pepper to taste

Sauté onion, leek, celery and bacon in a saucepan. Add squash and broth and simmer until squash is softened. Stir in cream, honey, salt and pepper.

Process soup in batches in a blender. Serve hot or cold. Garnish with chives, pancetta or smoked duck.

4 to 6 servings

Avocado Zucchini Soup

2	avocados, peeled and cut into chunks	1	(14-ounce) can chicken broth
2	zucchini, cut into chunks		Dash of white pepper
¼	onion, cut into chunks		Juice of 1 lime
			Yogurt or sour cream to taste

Combine avocados, zucchini, onion, broth, pepper and lime juice in a food processor and puree. Add yogurt or sour cream to desired consistency. Chill until very cold before serving.

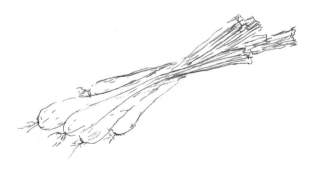

Okra Soup

	Ham bone or 2 small hocks	1½	teaspoons salt
1	(16-ounce) can tomatoes	½	teaspoon black pepper
2	(10-ounce) packages frozen okra	1	(16-ounce) package frozen butter beans
1	(16-ounce) package frozen yellow corn	2	tablespoons ketchup
		1	large onion, sliced
		3	medium potatoes, cut into chunks (optional)

Fill a large Dutch oven halfway with water. Add ham bone, bring to a boil and cook 1 hour. Remove meat from bone, discarding bone, skin and fat.

Add meat and all remaining ingredients to cooking broth. Cook over low heat for 1 to 1½ hours. Serve over rice or with cornbread.

8 to 10 servings

Some people prefer to use beef bones. My husband's aunt uses a combination of beef and ham bones. Fresh vegetables may be used, but cooking time should be lengthened to thoroughly cook vegetables. When using fresh okra, I add okra during the last 30 to 45 minutes of cooking time as okra cooks more quickly than the other vegetables.

During the summer in the Lowcountry, when okra and tomatoes are plentiful, okra soup has always been a favorite. There are many variations in the preparation such as the base of beef or ham and the addition of butter beans and corn. A popular way to serve the soup is in a flat soup bowl or over a plate of rice. Some call it okra soup, some okra gumbo, but all call it good eating, especially when served with cornbread.

Okra Soup

Chop a quarter peck of okra and skin a half-peck of tomatoes and place in a large soup pot. Add a shin or leg of beef and 10 quarts of cold water. Boil gently for 7 hours, skimming well.

Season with cayenne or black pepper and salt. A ham bone added with the beef is thought an improvement by some. Serve with rice.

A Carolina housewife, 1901

Carolina Rice Cookbook, compiled by Mrs. Samuel Stoney

Lena's Okra Gumbo

Freezes beautifully

1	ham with bone	3	(28-ounce) cans whole tomatoes
4	cups water		Salt and pepper to taste
2	large onions, chopped		Cooked white rice
3	(10-ounce) packages frozen okra		

Trim ham and cut meat from bone. Cut meat into large chunks. Measure 5 cups of ham chunks into a very large soup pot. Add ham bone, 4 cups water and onions. Boil, uncovered, 15 minutes. Add okra and tomatoes. Simmer 2 to 3 hours or until all ingredients are soft and fall apart.

Add water, if needed to reach desired consistency. Season with salt and pepper. Serve over or under rice.

12 to 16 cups

White Chili

For a buffet, serve White Chili with some or all of the following condiments: chopped tomatoes, chopped parsley, chopped black olives, guacamole, chopped green onions, sour cream, crumbled tortilla chips, salsa and hot corn bread muffins.

1	pound dried large white beans	2	teaspoons ground cumin
6	cups chicken broth	1½	teaspoons oregano
2	cloves garlic, minced	¼	teaspoon cayenne pepper
2	medium onions, chopped, divided	¼	teaspoon ground cloves
1	tablespoon vegetable oil	4	cups diced cooked chicken breast
2	(4-ounce) can chopped green chiles	3	cups grated Monterey Jack cheese

Soak beans in water overnight; drain. Combine beans, broth, garlic and 1 chopped onion in a large soup pot. Bring to a boil. Reduce heat and simmer 2 hours or until beans are very soft. Add more chicken broth, if needed, while cooking.

Heat oil in a skillet. Add remaining onion and sauté until tender. Add chiles, cumin, oregano, cayenne pepper and cloves. Mix well. Add mixture to soup pot with beans. Add chicken and continue to simmer 1 hour. Serve with cheese.

8 to 10 servings

Lentil Soup

1	pound dried lentils	¼	teaspoon thyme
1	medium onion, thinly sliced	2	quarts chicken broth
2	carrots, thinly sliced		Salt and pepper to taste
1	cup thinly sliced celery		Chopped, cooked chicken (optional)
1	large potato, peeled and grated	1	cup cooked rice (optional)
2	bay leaves		

Soak lentils overnight and drain. Combine soaked lentils with onion, carrots, celery, potato, bay leaves, thyme, broth, salt and pepper in a large pot. Simmer 2 to 3 hours.

Before serving, discard bay leaves. Add chicken and rice, if desired.

6 servings

Meatless Lentil Chili

6½	quarts water	8	ounces chili powder or to taste
3	tablespoons salt	4	ounces paprika
6	pounds dried lentils, rinsed	4	ounces ground cumin
½	pound onions, chopped	6	pounds canned dark red kidney beans
½	pound green bell peppers, chopped	6	pounds tomatoes, diced
4	ounces garlic powder	6	pounds canned tomato puree

Bring 6½ quarts water to a boil in a large soup pot. Add salt, lentils, onions, bell pepper, garlic powder, chili powder, paprika and cumin. Simmer 40 minutes or until lentils are tender.

Stir in kidney beans, tomatoes and tomato puree. Cook 20 to 30 minutes. Adjust seasonings, adding more chili powder if needed.

50 servings

This recipe is from Holy Apostles Episcopal Church in New York City.

It serves 50 people and is scaled down from their usual 1100 portions that is served Monday-Friday at their soup kitchen. They feed 1000 people each weekday!

Fred's Chili

1	teaspoon vegetable oil	¼	teaspoon cayenne
1	pound ground beef		pepper
2	cups chopped onion	5	teaspoons chili powder
4	cloves garlic	2	(16-ounce) cans red
2	green bell peppers,		kidney beans
	chopped	1	(28-ounce) can tomatoes
1	teaspoon salt		

Heat oil in a saucepan. Add beef and cook and stir until browned. Add onion, garlic and bell pepper and cook until tender. Mix in salt, cayenne pepper, chili powder, kidney beans and tomatoes. Simmer 1 hour.

4 to 6 servings

St. Michael's Oyster Roast Chili

15	pounds ground beef	6	(1¾-ounce) packages
1	extra large onion,		dry chili seasoning
	chopped		mix
1	(7-pound) can pinto	2	cups water
	beans, undrained		Chili powder to taste
1	(6½-pound) can tomato		Salt and pepper to
	sauce		taste
1	(6¼-pound) can		
	crushed tomatoes		

In batches, brown meat with onion and transfer to a large soup pot. Add beans, tomato sauce and tomatoes. Stir in seasoning mix and amount of water per package instructions plus 2 cups of water. Season with chili powder, salt and pepper. Simmer.

Serve with grated cheese and sour cream.

100 servings

Oyster roasts are a long-time outdoor Lowcountry tradition. They are held during the cooler months of the year, such as the months that have the letter "R" in their names.

This is when oysters are steamed outside over an open fire with a metal sheet and wet burlap sacks, or by a commercial steamer. After the oysters are cooked, they are piled on long tables with large holes in the center so that one may discard the oyster shells. The oysters are then pried open with oyster knives and dipped in melted butter or cocktail sauce.

St. Michael's Oyster Roast was the brainchild of Father Rick Belser and began in the late 1980's. Families have looked

Kansas City Steak Soup

Incredibly delicious! A hearty, filling soup.

½	cup butter or margarine	1	cup chopped onion
1	cup flour	1	cup chopped carrot
2	tablespoons beef bouillon	1	cup chopped celery
2	quarts water	1	cup chopped unpeeled white or red potato
1	(14½-ounce) can whole tomatoes	2	cups frozen mixed vegetables, or
1	pound lean ground beef or diced beef tenderloin		1 (16-ounce) package stew vegetables
2	cloves garlic, minced		Olive oil for sautéing
			Black pepper to taste

Melt butter in a large soup pot. Add flour and cook and stir over low heat until the roux is golden brown. Mix bouillon into water, then add to roux. Stir in tomatoes.

In a separate pan, sauté beef, garlic, onion, carrot, celery, potato and frozen vegetables in a small amount of olive oil. Add sautéed mixture to soup pot. Season with pepper; do not salt. Bring to a boil. Reduce heat and simmer about 1 hour. (We usually can't wait that long!!!)

Leftover roast beef, cut into small pieces, also works well.

Chicken Fajita Soup

Great for diet-conscious diners

2	chicken breasts, stewed and shredded	2	teaspoons chili powder
2	cups salsa	1	(16-ounce) can mexicorn, drained
1	(14½-ounce) can low fat, low sodium chicken broth	1	(16-ounce) can black beans, drained
		1¾	cups water

Combine all ingredients in a large pot and simmer for at least 30 minutes. For thinner soup, add more water.

About 10 cups

forward to this event as an anticipated gathering of the St. Michael's parish and guests. One year, a tourist couple rang the doorbell to the Rectory and wanted to know what was going on. They were immediately invited to join the party and happily entered in to the festivities.

Our joy is multiplied when we share our blessings and our lives with each other in Christ's name.

Add ¼ teaspoon curry powder (or more if you prefer) to any canned chicken soup for a zesty alternative.

Sweet Potato Vichyssoise

2½	pounds sweet potatoes		Salt to taste
1	cup rich chicken broth		White pepper to taste
1¾	cups sliced green		(optional)
	onion, mostly white	½	cup heavy cream
	part		Chopped fresh chives
4-5	cups rich chicken broth		for garnish
	(more if desired)		

Preheat oven to 400 degrees.

Roast potatoes in oven for 1 hour or until soft. Meanwhile, combine 1 cup chicken broth and green onions in a large saucepan. Simmer 15 minutes or until tender. Cool potatoes until able to handle. Scoop out pulp to equal at least 3 cups. Place pulp in a food processor along with green onions and broth from saucepan. Puree and return mixture to saucepan.

Add 4 cups chicken broth to saucepan. Simmer a few minutes longer. Add extra broth if soup is too thick. Season with salt and pepper. Refrigerate until chilled.

To serve, stir in cream and garnish with chives.

6 to 8 servings

Mushroom Bisque

4	tablespoons butter	4	cups chicken
8	ounces fresh		consommé
	mushrooms, sliced		Salt to taste
⅓	cup finely chopped	½	teaspoon black pepper
	onion	2	cups heavy cream
1	tablespoon fresh lemon	¼	cup dry sherry
	juice		Chopped fresh parsley
3	tablespoons flour		for garnish

Melt butter in a saucepan. Add mushrooms and onion and sauté 4 to 5 minutes, stirring constantly. Sprinkle with lemon juice and blend in flour. Gradually stir in consommé. Season with salt and pepper. Cook and stir until mixture is slightly thickened.

Add cream and sherry. Cook until thoroughly heated. Sprinkle with parsley and serve immediately.

12 servings

Corn Bisque with Red Bell Pepper and Rosemary

3	tablespoons butter	½	pound sausage links, quartered lengthwise, sliced and browned (optional)
2	cups chopped onion		
½	cup diced carrot		
½	cup diced celery		
5½	cups frozen corn, thawed and drained	1	cup half-and-half
1	teaspoon rosemary	2	cups frozen corn, thawed and drained
¼	teaspoon cayenne pepper	1	red bell pepper, chopped and sautéed
6	cups chicken broth		

Melt butter in a soup pot. Add onion, carrot and celery and sauté 3 minutes. Add 5½ cups corn, rosemary and cayenne pepper. Sauté 2 minutes. Stir in broth. Bring to a boil. Reduce heat to medium-low and simmer 30 minutes or until vegetables are tender and liquid is slightly reduced.

Working in batches, puree soup in a blender. Return soup to pot and add browned sausage. Mix in half-and-half and 2 cups corn. Season to taste. Add sautéed bell pepper.

Cold Zucchini Soup

4	medium zucchini, chopped	1	tablespoon chopped fresh dill
4	cups chicken broth	1	(8-ounce) container regular or low-fat sour cream
1	bunch green onions, chopped		
1	teaspoon salt		Chopped fresh chives for garnish
1	teaspoon white pepper		
2	(8-ounce) packages regular or low-fat cream cheese, softened		

Combine zucchini, broth, green onions, salt and white pepper in a saucepan. Cook over medium-high heat for 20 minutes, stirring occasionally. Add cream cheese and dill. Puree soup in a food processor or blender. Cover and chill 8 hours.

Mix in sour cream and chill 2 hours longer. Garnish with chives and serve.

6 to 8 servings

Portuguese Stone Soup

8	cups chicken broth	½	head savoy cabbage, coarsely chopped
1	pound kielbasa, diced	1	pound turnips, diced
1	(16-ounce) can kidney beans	2	carrots, diced
1	pound russet potatoes, diced	2	leeks, chopped
1	(14½-ounce) can diced tomatoes	4	cloves garlic, minced
		1	bay leaf

Combine all ingredients in a large pot. Simmer 2 hours.

Cold Tomato, Cucumber and Avocado Soup

Cream can be omitted, if desired, and the soup is still delicious.

4	tablespoons butter	4	cups peeled and chopped cucumber
1	cup chopped onion	4	cups chicken broth
¼	cup flour		Salt and pepper to taste
4	cups peeled and chopped tomatoes	1	ripe avocado
		1	cup heavy cream

Melt butter in a saucepan. Add onion and sauté until softened. Blend in flour. Whisk in tomato. Add cucumber, broth, salt and pepper. Simmer 25 minutes. Puree soup in a blender. Strain and refrigerate.

When soup is chilled, peel and chop avocado and add to chilled soup. Stir in cream and refrigerate until chilled.

8 servings

Cold Asparagus Soup

1 (12-ounce) can
   asparagus, undrained
1 (10¾-ounce) can beef
   broth

1 (8-ounce) container
   sour cream

Combine all ingredients in a blender and puree. Chill at least 1 to 2 hours.

4 servings

You may substitute low-fat sour cream for regular. So easy! So good!

Cold Cucumber Soup

1 pound cucumbers,
   peeled and chopped
1 (10¾-ounce) can
   condensed cream of
   chicken soup

1 (8-ounce) container
   sour cream
¼ large onion, chopped
   Salt to taste
   Worcestershire sauce to
   taste

Combine all ingredients in a blender or food processor and puree. Chill before servings.

4 servings

Cold Buttermilk Cucumber Soup

1 medium cucumber,
   finely diced
1 tablespoon chopped
   fresh dill, or
   ½ teaspoon dried

1 tablespoon Dijon
   mustard
1 teaspoon salt
1 teaspoon sugar
4 cups buttermilk

Combine all ingredients. Chill thoroughly.

For a luncheon dish, add 1 pound cooked and chopped shrimp. Serve with hot biscuits.

Olga's Gazpacho

This is the way my Spanish daughter-in-law makes Gazpacho. She learned this traditional Spanish recipe from her mother in Jerez, Spain. She says one must use a blender, not a food processor.

4	medium to large tomatoes	3	tablespoons olive oil, preferably Spanish olive oil
2	green bell peppers, seeded and veins removed	2	tablespoons light red wine vinegar
¼	cucumber, peeled and seeded if desired		Salt and pepper to taste
½	medium onion		Chopped tomato, onion, cucumber and parsley for garnish
1-3	cloves garlic or to taste		

Cut tomatoes, bell peppers, cucumber, and onion into pieces that will fit into a blender. Place about 2 tomatoes in blender. Add bell peppers, cucumber, onion and garlic. Add remainder of tomatoes and blend well. Add oil and vinegar. Season with salt and pepper. Blend well. Work in batches, if necessary. Thin soup with up to ½ cup water or ice if desired.

Cover and refrigerate for at least 2 hours. Garnish as desired with chopped vegetables.

About 4 cups

Crusty bread, such as French or Italian, can be added to the soup while blending. Use about 2 slices of bread or ¾ to 1 hard roll and adjust water as needed.

Herbed Tomato Soup

½	cup unsalted butter	3	tablespoons tomato paste
2	tablespoons olive oil	⅓	cup all-purpose flour
1	large onion, thinly sliced	4	cups chicken broth, divided
4	sprigs fresh thyme, or 1 teaspoon dried	1	teaspoon sugar
	Salt and freshly ground black pepper to taste	1	cup heavy cream
2½	pounds fresh tomatoes, peeled and cored, or 1 (35-ounce) can, undrained	4	tablespoons butter Croutons for garnish

Melt ½ cup butter with olive oil in a soup pot. Add onion, thyme, salt and pepper and sauté, stirring occasionally, until onion is softened. Stir in tomatoes and tomato paste. Simmer 10 minutes.

Place flour in a small mixing bowl. Blend in about ⅓ cup of the broth. Add flour mixture to soup pot along with remainder of broth. Simmer 30 minutes, stirring frequently to prevent scorching.

Puree soup in a food processor or blender and return to pot. Heat and add sugar and cream. Simmer, stirring occasionally, for 5 minutes. Swirl in 4 tablespoons butter. Serve hot or cold. Garnish with croutons.

Add milk and basil to a can of tomato soup to enhance the flavor.

She-Crab Soup
A Charleston favorite!

1	cup white crabmeat	½	cup heavy cream
2	tablespoons butter	½	teaspoon Worcestershire sauce
1	small onion, chopped	2	teaspoons flour
¼	teaspoon mace	4	tablespoons dry sherry
2	stalks celery, chopped	⅛	teaspoon pepper
¼	teaspoon salt		
2	cups milk		

Place crab in double boiler; add butter, onion, salt, pepper, mace and celery. Let simmer until onion and celery are tender. Add milk, cream and Worcestershire sauce; stir. Thicken with paste made of flour and water. Add sherry. Cook slowly over low heat for 25 minutes. Additional sherry may be added to each serving if desired.

4 to 6 servings

Kevin's Sweet Potato Apple Soup

4	large onions, diced	2	cups apple juice
	Olive oil for sautéing	2	(29-ounce) cans chicken
3-4	cloves garlic, minced		broth
4	sweet potatoes, peeled	1	tablespoon thyme
	and diced		Salt and pepper to
3	McIntosh apples, diced		taste
2	Granny Smith apples,		Parmesan cheese and
	diced		nutmeg for garnish

Sauté onions in olive oil in a Dutch oven. Add garlic and sauté until browned. Stir in sweet potatoes, apples, apple juice and broth. Bring to a boil. Reduce heat and simmer until potatoes and apples are softened. Puree mixture in a food processor or blender and return to pot.

Add thyme to soup and simmer 15 minutes. Season with salt and pepper. Add more apple juice if soup is too thick. Serve soup hot sprinkled with Parmesan cheese and nutmeg.

4 to 6 servings

Chilled Beet and Yogurt Soup
"It's a beautiful pink."

¼	cup minced onion	¼	teaspoon black pepper
1	(16-ounce) can sliced	¼	teaspoon dried dill
	beets, undrained	1	cup plain yogurt
1	tablespoon sugar		Yogurt or sour cream
¼	cup lemon juice		and dill for garnish

Puree onion in a blender. Add undrained beets, sugar, lemon juice, pepper and dill to blender and blend until smooth. Stir in yogurt by hand or using low speed of blender.

Chill thoroughly before serving. Top each serving with a dollop of yogurt or sour cream and a light sprinkling of dill.

Choir Punch

St. Michael's choir enjoys this punch on special occasions.

1	(2-liter) bottle diet white grape soda	1	(64-ounce) bottle 100% white grape juice Ice as needed

Combine soda and juice in a punch bowl. Add ice to chill.

About 1 gallon

Hot Spiced Tea

2	quarts hot brewed tea	½	cup freshly squeezed lemon juice
1¾	cups sugar or to taste		
½	cup boiling water	1¼	cups orange juice
2	tablespoons whole cloves	2	cups pineapple juice

Combine tea with sugar and stir until sugar dissolves. Pour boiling water over cloves and let steep 15 minutes.

Combine tea, cloves with water, lemon juice, orange juice and pineapple juice in a saucepan. Bring to a boil.

Strain tea. If clear tea is desired, strain through a double-layer of cheesecloth. Serve tea hot with thin slices of lemon.

3 quarts

Minnie's Sherbet Punch

1	(46-ounce) can pineapple juice	1	(1-liter) bottle ginger ale
1	(46-ounce) can orange juice	1	gallon orange sherbet

Combine all ingredients in a punch bowl. Add ice. Serve immediately.

80 punch glass servings

Hot Punch

Apple cider   **Cinnamon sticks**
Cranberry juice

Heat equal parts of apple cider and cranberry juice in a saucepan. Stir in cinnamon sticks. Serve in a punch bowl.

For decoration, stick cloves in an orange and place in the punch bowl.

Grapefruit Slush

2	(46-ounce) cans grapefruit juice	2	cups water
2	cups sugar	½-¾	teaspoon oil of peppermint

Combine all ingredients and stir until sugar dissolves. Freeze in 2 containers. Thaw mixture slightly and serve from a punch bowl when slushy. Mixture is too sweet when completely melted.

15 servings

Jim Isle Punch

This punch cools you off after a long day in the boat or swinging off the rope swing across the creek.

1	cup dark rum (we prefer Goslings Black Seal)	2	cups ginger ale
			Juice of 1 lime
¾	cup orange juice	1	lime, cut into wedges for garnish

Combine all ingredients except lime wedges in a pitcher.

To serve, pour mixture over crushed ice in glasses. Garnish with lime wedges.

6 servings

Christmas Coffee Punch for Rectory Drop-In

2 gallons strong hot coffee
1-2 cups sugar
2 quarts heavy cream, whipped
4 quarts vanilla ice cream, softened

2-3 teaspoons vanilla extract or to taste
2-3 teaspoons almond extract or to taste
1 pint heavy cream, whipped for topping
Cinnamon to taste

Combine hot coffee and sugar and stir until dissolved. Refrigerate until cooled completely or up to 24 hours.

When ready to serve, divide coffee between 2 punch bowls. Fold in 2 quarts whipped cream and ice cream. Stir in extracts. Float whipped pint of cream on top and sprinkle with cinnamon.

40 servings

The Reverend and Mrs. Belser began having a drop-in at the Rectory after our 10:30 service on a Sunday near Christmas. St. Michaelites and visitors enjoy this open house around the holidays. Children have their special table in the breakfast room with punch and candy canes!

Mocha Coffee Punch

4 quarts boiling water
1 (8-ounce) jar instant coffee
8 (1-ounce) squares unsweetened chocolate, melted

2⅔ cups sugar
4 gallons vanilla ice cream or more
8 quarts milk

Combine water, coffee, chocolate and sugar. Stir until mixed. If making ahead, refrigerate until ready to serve.

To serve, place 1 gallon ice cream and 2 quarts milk in a punch bowl. Slowly pour one-fourth of coffee mixture over ice cream and milk. Blend well. As punch bowl empties, repeat this step 3 times.

160 servings

This recipe is traditionally used at many of St. Michael's parties and receptions.

This was called "The Recipe" because it was so popular and also to disguise the fact that it was spiked. Mrs. Karl Kilgus served it at my sister's wedding in Bamberg, S.C. Because Bamberg is Baptist country, folks in the know asked for "The Recipe" or "That Punch." I've served it all over the world since then and everyone always asks for "The Recipe."

"The Recipe" (Champagne Punch)

1	quart cranberry juice cocktail	2	cups brandy
1	(6-ounce) can frozen orange juice concentrate	2	(750 ml) bottles white champagne (no need to use expensive champagne)
1	quart pineapple juice		

Combine all ingredients in a punch bowl. Float an ice ring on top.

30 punch cups or 50 champagne glasses

Make an ice ring out of ingredients used in the punch. Place pineapple slices with a maraschino cherry in the center of each in the bottom of a ring mold. Pour liquid over top and freeze. It is wise to make 2 or 3 rings to last for a party.

Open House Punch

1	(750 ml) bottle bourbon, chilled	1	(6-ounce) can frozen lemonade concentrate
¾	cup fresh or bottled lemon juice, chilled	3	(1-liter) bottles lemon-lime soda, chilled
1	(6-ounce) can frozen orange juice concentrate		Red food coloring (optional) Orange and lemon slices for garnish

Combine bourbon, lemon juice and concentrates in a punch bowl. Mix in soda. Add drops of food coloring as desired. Stir.

Float a block of ice in punch or add ice cubes. Garnish with orange or lemon slices.

Champagne Cocktail

	Champagne	¼	teaspoon Cointreau
1	teaspoon crème de cassis		

Fill a flute half full with champagne. Add crème de cassis and Cointreau. Fill to top with more champagne.

1 serving

Kahlúa

4	cups water	1	liter vodka
4	cups sugar	½	liter brandy
½	cup instant coffee	1	tablespoon vanilla

Heat water. Add sugar and coffee and heat until dissolved. Remove from heat. Stir in vodka, brandy and vanilla.

Use immediately or pour into bottles and seal with a cork. Flavor improves with age.

5 (16-ounce) bottles

Toasted Almond

2	cups vanilla ice cream	½	teaspoon almond extract
¾	cup Kahlúa		Freshly ground nutmeg
½	cup crushed ice		

Blend ice cream, Kahlúa and ice in a blender. Add almond extract and process until well blended.

Pour into large decorative glasses. Dust with nutmeg.

2 servings

Iceberg Slush

2 (6-ounce) cans frozen lemonade concentrate	1½ cups pineapple juice
2 cups water	2 cups white rum

Combine all ingredients in a plastic milk jug or other container. Freeze 6 hours.

To serve, remove from freezer and shake or stir until slushy.

14 servings

Only the poorest whites, slaves and frontiersmen drank water in early South Carolina. The average South Carolinian drank a mixture of rum and water, spruce beer or cider. Madeira was also a favorite.

My Dad's Drop Dead Punch

Be careful! It's potent!

1 part bourbon	2 parts sparkling white grape juice

Pour ingredients over a block of ice in a punch bowl.

Legare Street Punch

1 (750 ml) bottle Cointreau	1 (6-ounce) can pineapple juice concentrate
1 (750 ml) bottle vodka	
1 (6-ounce) can orange juice concentrate	3 (1-liter) bottles club soda

Blend all ingredients except club soda in a punch bowl. Add club soda just before serving.

Garnish with orange slices decorated with cranberries and studded with cloves.

Tom Palmer's 250th Anniversary Wine Punch

1   (750ml) bottle Claret
    (if not available,
    Merlot or Cabernet
    may be used)
1   cup orange juice
1   cup pineapple juice
2   lemons, thinly sliced
1   orange, thinly sliced

Mix wine, orange juice and pineapple juice. Pour over ice in a punch bowl. Add lemon and orange slices.

12 servings

Ingredients may be increased as needed. This was served at St. Michael's 250th Anniversary Celebration and was a big hit.

The ingredients for the punch were listed in an 1887 history of St. Michael's, written by George Holmes. He was a former senior warden at the church.

Jasmine Pointe Eggnog

12 eggs, separated
2   cups fine sugar
1   quart milk
2   quarts heavy cream
1   quart bourbon
¼   cup dark rum
2   cups Cognac
    Grated nutmeg

Beat the egg yolks until thick, add sugar and stir. With a wire whisk, beat in the milk and the cream. Add the bourbon, rum and Cognac, stirring constantly. Beat the egg whites until stiff. Fold into mixture. Sprinkle with nutmeg.

16 servings

My Mimi's Iced Tea

2	quarts boiling water	½	cup Country Time
14	Lipton tea bags		lemonade
½	cup sugar		

Pour 2 quarts of boiling water over 14 individual Lipton tea bags. Cover and let brew for 8 minutes.

Add approximately ½ cup sugar and ½ cup Country Time lemonade to a one-gallon container. Add tea and additional water to make 1 gallon of tea.

Tea tastes best if left in the refrigerator overnight.

Mint Julep

I have often chuckled to myself after being asked by tourists what time we drink mint juleps—as if the whole town of Charleston closed down at 3:00 and we went home to enjoy the potent concoction while enjoying our joggling boards on our piazzas.

For each serving:

3	mint sprigs	2	ounces fine bourbon
1	teaspoon sugar		Crushed ice
2	teaspoons water	1	sprig mint

In each julep glass place the sugar and water. Mix together to make a syrup. Add 3 mint sprigs and muddle by turning a cocktail spoon around so that the bowl of the spoon grinds the mint into the syrup mixture. Fill the glass with crushed ice, taking care not to touch the outside of the glass. Pour in bourbon. Stir vigorously to form a frosting on the outside of the glass. Garnish with remaining mint sprig. Serve immediately.

Salads & Such

"...the Garden of Eden."

Children in Washington Park

Easter dresses, grosgrain ribbons, baskets of eggs,
white shoes. There are many places for egg hiding
in Washington Park, just across the street from
St. Michael's. The park has hosted generations of
St. Michael's fellowship activities. By the way,
in 1791, when he worshiped at St. Michael's,
George Washington sat in Pew #43.

"If we walk in the light, as he is in the light,
we have fellowship with one another and the blood
of Jesus Christ his son cleanseth us from all sin."
I John 1:8

Low Calories Buttermilk Dressing

2	cups buttermilk	1	teaspoon onion powder
2	cups low-calorie mayonnaise	½	teaspoon garlic powder
		½	teaspoon black pepper

Combine all ingredients and blend well. Store in refrigerator.

4 cups

Salads & Such

Mustard Vinaigrette Salad Dressing

½	cup vegetable oil	3	cloves garlic, minced
⅓	cup lemon juice	½	teaspoon salt
2	teaspoons Dijon mustard	½	teaspoon black pepper

Combine all ingredients in a jar and shake to mix. Serve over lettuce salads with tomato for garnish.

About 1 cup

Sherry Vinaigrette

½	cup balsamic vinegar	1	teaspoon Italian herbs
1	teaspoon coarsely ground black pepper	⅓	cup sugar
1	clove garlic, crushed and minced, or 1 teaspoon garlic powder	2	tablespoons sherry
		1	cup olive oil

Combine all ingredients except oil. Slowly whisk in oil.

2 cups

Italian Salad

Use Tomato Basil Dressing drizzled over a platter of freshly sliced cucumbers, tomatoes and sweet onions.

Salad

3	cups Romaine or spring greens	½	cup crumbled feta cheese
1	tomato, chopped, or ½ cup grape tomatoes	½	cup thinly sliced green onions
½	cup toasted pine nuts		

Tomato Basil Dressing

½	cup wine or balsamic vinegar	1	clove garlic, crushed and minced, or 1 teaspoon garlic powder
2	fresh tomatoes, peeled or ½ cup canned tomato purée	½	teaspoon Italian herbs
⅓	cup sugar	1	tablespoon basil
1	teaspoon coarsely ground black pepper	1	cup olive oil

Combine all salad ingredients in a bowl. Toss with desired amount of Tomato Basil Dressing.

To make dressing, process all dressing ingredients except oil in a blender. With blender running, add oil slowly. Store in refrigerator but bring to room temperature before using.

4 salad servings, 2 cups dressing

Jade Delight Salad Dressing

½	cup rice vinegar	½	teaspoon dried red pepper flakes
⅓	cup sugar	1	tablespoon cilantro
½	tablespoon sesame oil	1	tablespoon basil
1	tablespoon soy sauce	¾	cup peanut oil
1	teaspoon grated ginger		
1	clove garlic, crushed and minced, or 1 teaspoon garlic powder		

Process all ingredients except oil in a blender. With blender running, add oil slowly. Store in refrigerator but bring to room temperature before using.

2 cups

Miss Libby's Mayonnaise

Great on cucumber and tomato sandwiches.

2	egg yolks	1	teaspoon garlic salt
2	tablespoons prepared mustard	1	teaspoon salt
2	cups vegetable oil	½	teaspoon black pepper
1	teaspoon onion flakes	12	dashes Tabasco sauce
		½	cup vinegar or to taste

Mix egg yolks and mustard to make a paste. Blend in oil slowly until mixture thickens. Mix in onion flakes, garlic salt, salt, black pepper and Tabasco sauce. Mix in vinegar, adding a little at a time, to taste. Store in refrigerator.

For a lower fat version, use low-fat store-bought mayonnaise. Add spices and vinegar (balsamic vinegar adds extra flavor).

Poppy Seed Dressing

¾	cup sugar	1½	tablespoons poppy seeds
1	teaspoon dry mustard	1	cup vegetable oil (not olive oil)
1	teaspoon salt		
⅓	cup white vinegar		
¼	cup chopped onion		

Process all ingredients except oil in a blender. With blender running, add oil slowly. Store in refrigerator.

2 cups

Cate's Blue Cheese Dressing

½	cup blue cheese	⅛	teaspoon seasoning salt
3	tablespoons mayonnaise	⅛	teaspoon lemon pepper
½	cup red wine vinegar	⅛	teaspoon Greek seasoning
¾	cup olive oil	⅛	teaspoon dried parsley flakes
¼	teaspoon basil		

Combine all ingredients in a jar and shake to mix. Store in refrigerator but bring to room temperature before using.

6 servings

Divine on top of a thin slice of Vidalia onion and a thick slice of summer's best tomato.

Grandmother's Blue Cheese Dressing

1 quart real mayonnaise (not salad dressing type)	Scant 1 cup half-and-half
	Dash of garlic powder or to taste
8 ounces blue cheese	Dash of salt
1 cup buttermilk	Dash of white pepper

Combine all ingredients. Store in a jar in refrigerator.

1¾ quart

Caesar Salad

Dressing

1-2 cloves garlic	⅛-¼ teaspoon salt
3-4 anchovy fillets	¼-½ teaspoon mustard powder
1 tablespoon Parmesan cheese	1 teaspoon sugar
½-1 teaspoon anchovy oil (from can of anchovies)	⅓-½ cup virgin olive oil
	2-4 tablespoons freshly squeezed lemon juice
1-2 dashes Worcestershire sauce	1 coddled egg yolk
1-2 dashes Tabasco sauce	1-2 tablespoons white vinegar
¼-½ teaspoon black pepper	

Salad

Romaine lettuce	Croutons
Parmesan cheese	

To make dressing, pulverize garlic, anchovy fillets and Parmesan cheese with a mortar and pestle. Add anchovy oil, Worcestershire sauce, Tabasco sauce, pepper, salt, mustard and sugar. Pulverize and mix well. Add olive oil, lemon juice, egg yolk and vinegar. Mix well.

To prepare salad, wash and dry lettuce and break into small pieces. Place lettuce in a bowl. Add desired amount of dressing and toss. Sprinkle with Parmesan cheese and croutons. Serve immediately.

4 to 6 servings

French Salad

Salad
3	cups torn Romaine lettuce
½	cup sliced raw mushrooms

¼	cup golden raisins
¼	cup dry roasted peanuts
	Goat cheese to taste

Dressing
½	cup olive oil
2	tablespoons sesame seeds

¼	cup lemon juice
1	teaspoon parsley

Combine all salad ingredients in a bowl. Toss salad with dressing.

To make dressing, combine oil and sesame seeds in a saucepan and cook until seeds start to turn golden. Remove from heat and cool 10 minutes. Mix in lemon juice and parsley.

6 servings

Janet's Frozen Tomato Salad

1	(28-ounce) can crushed tomatoes
1¾	cups mayonnaise
	Grated onion to taste

Worcestershire sauce to taste
Salt and pepper to taste

Combine all ingredients and place in a square or oblong dish. Freeze.

Just before serving, remove from freezer. Cut into squares and serve on lettuce leaves. For garnish, top each serving with a dollop of mayonnaise and a dash of paprika.

8 servings

Ice was not used for the preservation of food in Charleston until 1799, when a hotel-keeper opened an ice depot.

Pretzel Salad

Crust

2	cups coarsely crushed pretzels	¾	cup margarine, melted
		3	tablespoons sugar

Filling

1	(8-ounce) package cream cheese	2	cups frozen non-dairy whipped topping, thawed
1	cup sugar		

Topping

2	(3-ounce) packages strawberry jello	2	(10-ounce) packages frozen strawberries
		2	cups boiling water

Preheat oven to 400 degrees.

Combine all crust ingredients and press into a 9x13-inch baking dish. Bake 8 to 10 minutes. Cool.

To make filling, blend cream cheese and sugar together. Fold in whipped topping. Spread filling over crust.

For topping, combine jello, strawberries and boiling water. Stir until jello dissolves. Cool in refrigerator 10 minutes. Pour cooled topping over filling. Refrigerate until set.

Mom's Easy Aspic

1	(46-ounce) can vegetable juice	1	envelope unflavored gelatin
1	(5.5-ounce) can vegetable juice	¼	cup water
3	(3-ounce) packages lemon jello		Dash of Worcestershire sauce
			Dash of garlic powder

Pour both cans of vegetable juice into a saucepan. Heat until hot, but not boiling. Stir in jello until dissolved.

Dissolve unflavored gelatin in ¼ cup water. Add 2 to 3 tablespoons of hot juice mixture to gelatin, then slowly add to juice mixture. Season juice mixture with Worcestershire sauce and garlic powder. Pour into a round mold or square glass dish. Refrigerate until firm.

Garnish mold or individual servings with mayonnaise and parsley.

Ruthie's Tomato Aspic

1	(46-ounce) can vegetable juice	1	(3-ounce) package lemon jello
1	onion, chopped	3	envelopes unflavored gelatin
2	tablespoons Worcestershire sauce	½	cup cold water
12	drops Tabasco sauce or to taste		Chopped vegetables of choice

Combine juice, onion, Worcestershire sauce and Tabasco sauce in a saucepan. Bring to a boil and cook 10 to 15 minutes, stirring occasionally. Remove from heat.

Dissolve lemon jello and unflavored gelatin in ½ cup cold water. Stir gelatin liquid into hot juice mixture until gelatin completely dissolves. Pour mixture into an 8- or 9-inch glass dish or greased mold. Chill until partially set.

Add chopped vegetables and stir to mix. Chill until completely set. Serve on lettuce with mayonnaise on the side. Sprinkle mayonnaise with paprika for color.

This aspic is good with the addition of any of these vegetables: olives, celery, bell pepper, artichoke hearts, hearts of palm or whatever vegetable you prefer!

Salads & Such

Dublin Potato Salad

1	(12-ounce) can corned beef	½-1	tablespoon pickle juice or to taste
3	medium to large potatoes	2	cups finely shredded cabbage
1	teaspoon salt	1	teaspoon celery seed
2	tablespoons rice vinegar	2	sweet dill pickles, chopped
1	tablespoon prepared mustard		

Refrigerate can of corned beef the night before preparation.

Boil potatoes with salt 30 to 40 minutes; drain. Cube potatoes and place in a bowl. Combine vinegar, mustard and pickle juice and drizzle over potatoes while they are still hot.

Cube corned beef. Add beef to potatoes along with cabbage, celery seed and chopped pickles. Toss and serve.

6 to 8 servings

Cole Slaw

3 cups thinly sliced
  cabbage
1 medium onion, chopped
1 green bell pepper,
  chopped
1 teaspoon mustard seed

½ teaspoon salt
1 teaspoon celery seed
¼ cup sugar
½ cup vinegar
¼ cup mayonnaise

Combine all ingredients except mayonnaise and let stand
for 1 hour or more. Drain well. Stir in mayonnaise.

Black Olive Salad

½ cup zesty Italian dressing
½ cup water
1 cup dry instant rice
½ cup chopped black
  olives
½ cup chopped green
  onions

½ cup chopped cucumber
½ cup chopped canned
  mushrooms, drained
1 (17-ounce) can Le Seur
  peas, or 1 (16-ounce)
  package frozen
½ cup mayonnaise

Bring dressing and water to a boil. Mix in rice. Stir in olives,
onions, cucumber, mushrooms, peas and mayonnaise.
Refrigerate until chilled. Best made the day before serving.

Friendship Salad

3-4 cups chopped lettuce
2 tablespoons crumbled
  feta or goat cheese
½ artichoke heart

1 tablespoon black or
  English walnuts
  Gerard's raspberry
  dressing to taste

Combine all ingredients and toss.

2 servings

Granny Smith Apple and Blue Cheese Salad

2	large Granny Smith apples, peeled if desired Lemon juice	1	(4- to 6-ounce) package crumbled blue cheese
2	heads Boston or Bibb lettuce	1	cup chopped walnuts or pecans Poppy seed dressing

Thinly slice apples and sprinkle with lemon juice to prevent browning. Drain juice before using apples. Wash and dry lettuce and tear into bite-size pieces.

Combine drained apples, lettuce, blue cheese and walnuts. Drizzle with dressing and toss.

6 to 8 servings

From the fruit of his lips a man is filled with good things as surely as the work of his hands rewards him.

~ Proverbs 12:14

Salads & Such

Watermelon and Avocado Salad

Great for brunch or an outdoor summer party.

1	small red onion, thinly sliced		Juice of 1 orange
2	tablespoons red wine vinegar	2	teaspoons virgin olive oil
2	small or 1 large avocado Juice of 1 lime	1	cup loosely packed fresh cilantro Salt and freshly ground black pepper to taste
4-5	cups seeded and cubed watermelon		

Combine onion and vinegar in a nonreactive container. Cover and marinate in refrigerator several hours or overnight.

Peel and cut avocados into 1-inch chunks. Toss with lime juice to prevent browning. Combine avocado, watermelon, orange juice, olive oil and cilantro. Drain onion and add to salad. Toss and season with salt and pepper.

6 to 8 servings

Lemon Greek Salad

⅓ cup vegetable oil
  Juice and zest of 1 lemon
½ teaspoon dried oregano
¼ teaspoon garlic salt
¼ teaspoon black pepper
1 (6-ounce) can pitted
  black olives, drained
1 medium cucumber,
  scored and sliced

1 medium sweet green
  bell pepper, cut into
  1-inch pieces
12 cherry tomatoes, halved
4 ounces feta cheese,
  crumbled
1 small head iceberg
  lettuce, torn

Combine oil, lemon juice and zest, oregano, garlic salt and pepper in a bowl. Add olives, cucumber, bell pepper, tomatoes and cheese. Mix well, cover and chill.

To serve, arrange lettuce in a serving bowl. Top with marinated vegetable mixture. Toss gently, if desired.

Oriental Slaw

½ cup vegetable oil
2 tablespoons sugar
3 tablespoons white
  vinegar
1 teaspoon salt
½ teaspoon black pepper
1 tablespoon chicken
  granules

1 head cabbage, outer
  leaves used, shredded
1-2 green onions, chopped
½ cup slivered almonds
2 tablespoons sesame
  seeds, toasted
½ cup rice noodles

Combine oil, sugar, vinegar, salt, pepper and chicken flavoring in a blender. Blend to mix. Place cabbage and onions in a bowl. Add oil mixture and toss. Add almonds, sesame seeds and rice noodles. Serve.

Broccoli Carbonara

1   **bunch broccoli, chopped plus an equal amount of chopped cauliflower**
½   **cup raisins, soaked in warm water and drained**
¾   **cup mayonnaise**

1   **tablespoon vinegar**
1   **tablespoon sugar**
2-3 **green onions, sliced**
1   **(3-ounce) package slivered almonds, toasted**
¼   **cup bacon bits**

Combine all ingredients except bacon bits. Sprinkle bacon bits on top and serve.

8 servings

Salads & Such

"Hot" Spinach Salad with Goat Cheese

1   **(6-ounce) package sliced portobella mushrooms**
½   **medium-size yellow or white onion**
¼   **cup olive oil**
¾   **cup Greek olives**
6   **cherry tomatoes, sliced, or 1 medium tomato, sliced**

3   **tablespoons balsamic vinegar**
1   **medium bunch fresh spinach, rinsed and drained, stems discarded**
¼   **cup goat cheese**
    Salt and pepper to taste

Cut mushrooms in half if large. Sauté mushrooms and onion in oil until tender. Add olives, tomato slices and vinegar. Cook over low heat for 10 to 15 minutes.

Place spinach on a serving platter. Top with pats of goat cheese. Pour mushroom mixture over top. Season with salt and pepper and extra balsamic vinegar to taste. Serve immediately.

4 servings

Seven Layer Salad

3	cups chopped iceberg lettuce	2	tablespoons mayonnaise
1	cup frozen green peas	2	ounces Cheddar cheese, grated
¼	cup chopped onion	2	slices bacon, cooked crisp and crumbled
½	cup chopped celery		
½	cup nonfat plain yogurt	2	hard-cooked eggs, sliced

In a medium casserole dish, layer lettuce, peas, onion and celery. Mix together yogurt and mayonnaise and spread over vegetables. Top with layers of cheese, bacon and egg slices. Cover and refrigerate at least 8 hours.

8 to 10 servings

Overnight Vegetable Salad

1	(16-ounce) can tiny green peas, drained	¾	cup finely chopped celery
1	(16-ounce) can French-style green beans, drained	2	tablespoons chopped pimento
		¾	cup sugar
1	(11-ounce) can white shoepeg corn, drained	½	cup vegetable oil
		½	cup white wine vinegar
1	medium onion, finely chopped	½	teaspoon salt
		½	teaspoon black pepper

Combine peas, beans, corn, onion, celery and pimento in a large bowl.

In a saucepan, mix sugar, oil, vinegar, salt and pepper. Heat and stir until sugar dissolves. Pour over vegetables.

Cover and refrigerate overnight. Leftovers can be stored several days in refrigerator.

10 to 12 servings

Marinated Vegetable Salad

1	pound broccoli	½	cup minced fresh parsley
1	small head cauliflower	⅓	cup fresh lemon juice
1	(8½-ounce) can artichoke hearts, drained	1	teaspoon salt
		1	teaspoon sugar
½	(16-ounce) package frozen crinkle-cut carrots, cooked and drained	1	teaspoon oregano
		1	teaspoon basil
		1	teaspoon dried mustard
		¼	teaspoon freshly ground black pepper
1	large green bell pepper, cut into strips	⅔	cup oil
		1	(16-ounce) can black olives, drained
1	medium-size red onion, sliced and separated into rings	4	ounces blue cheese, crumbled

Separate broccoli and cauliflower into florets. Peel broccoli stem and cut into 1-inch pieces. Cook broccoli and cauliflower 5 to 7 minutes. Combine broccoli, cauliflower, artichoke hearts, carrots, bell pepper, onion and parsley in a large bowl.

In a separate bowl, combine lemon juice, salt, sugar, oregano, basil, mustard and pepper. Whisk in oil until smooth. Pour over vegetables.

Refrigerate at least 4 hours or preferably overnight, turning mixture occasionally. Just before serving, stir in olives and cheese.

8 servings

Salads & Such

Supreme Seafood Salad

The key is in the presentation!! Serve with hot crusty rolls.

2 heads Boston lettuce, washed and dried
3 heads endive, washed, dried and leaves separated
½ cup slivered celery, blanched 1 minute
2 tomatoes, peeled and cut into wedges
½ pound scallops
  White wine
1 pound fresh crabmeat
1 lobster tail, cooked and meat sliced

1 pound cooked and peeled shrimp
2 hard-cooked eggs, finely chopped
1 tablespoon chopped fresh chives
  Salt and pepper to taste
¼ cup thinly sliced green onions
1 bunch watercress, picked over and washed

Dressing

1 cup sour cream
1 cup mayonnaise
2 tablespoons horseradish sauce

¼ cup red or black caviar (optional)

Line a shallow serving bowl with Boston lettuce leaves, then line with endive. Arrange celery and tomato wedges on top.

Poach scallops in white wine until firm, drain and cool. Arrange scallops, crabmeat, lobster and shrimp over vegetables in serving bowl. Sprinkle with eggs, chives, salt and pepper. Pile green onions on top and place 2 bundles of watercress at either end.

Combine all dressing ingredients in a separate bowl.

To serve, pour dressing over salad at the table and toss.

14 servings

Walker's Crab and Shrimp Salad

Divine!

1	pound lump or backfin crabmeat, picked over	½-¾	cup mayonnaise
			Several dashes Worcestershire sauce
½	pound medium shrimp, cooked and peeled	2	tablespoons capers

Gently mix all ingredients together. Refrigerate at least 2 hours before serving.

4 to 6 servings

This salad is wonderful served on a bed of Boston lettuce with sliced tomatoes and crescent rolls.

Gorgeous Green Salad with Shrimp

Dressing

1	cup cottage cheese	1	clove garlic
2	cups salad oil	1	teaspoon peppercorns
½	medium onion		Large dash of cayenne pepper
⅔	cup white vinegar		
	Juice of 1 lemon		

Salad

2	avocados	1	head iceberg lettuce
2	pounds large shrimp, cooked and peeled	1	pound bacon, cut into thin strips and cooked crisp
1	bunch spinach		
1	head romaine lettuce		

Combine all dressing ingredients in a blender and process.

To prepare salad, peel and slice avocados. Combine avocados and shrimp in a large bowl. Pour dressing on top, cover and refrigerate overnight.

Wash and dry spinach and lettuces. Wrap leaves in a wet towel and refrigerate overnight.

When ready to serve, tear greens into bite-size pieces and add to avocado and shrimp mixture. Toss gently. Sprinkle with bacon.

8 to 10 servings

Old Fashioned Chicken Salad

This can be served as a main dish at a luncheon or as an appetizer served with crackers. Also makes delicious chicken salad sandwiches.

Chicken

3	pounds boneless, skinless chicken breast	1	medium onion, chopped
		2	teaspoons salt
½	cup butter	1	teaspoon black pepper
2	stalks celery, chopped	1	tablespoon poultry seasoning

Salad

	Prepared chicken	1	teaspoon salt
1	teaspoon sweet relish	1	teaspoon black pepper
1	cup minced celery	1	tablespoon heavy cream
½	cup minced onion	1	teaspoon prepared mustard
½	cup sour cream		
1	cup mayonnaise		

In a pot, combine all ingredients for preparing chicken. Add enough water to cover. Bring to a boil. Cook 30 minutes or until chicken is done. Remove chicken from pot. Cool and cut with a scissors into bite-size pieces.

To make salad, combine above prepared chicken with remaining salad ingredients. Mix well and serve.

10 to 12 servings

To make soup: Add peas and carrots, rice or pasta to chicken broth for a delicious soup.

Chicken Taco Salad

Dressing

1	medium avocado, peeled and sliced	1	clove garlic, minced
1	tablespoon fresh lemon juice	½	teaspoon sugar
½	cup sour cream	½	teaspoon chili powder
¼	cup vegetable oil	¼	teaspoon salt
		¼	teaspoon hot pepper sauce (optional)

Salad

½	medium head lettuce	¼	cup sliced green onions
2	cups cooked and cubed chicken	8	slices bacon, cooked and crumbled
1	tomato, seeded and chopped	¾	cup grated Cheddar cheese
½	cup sliced black olives	1	cup crushed corn chips

Combine all dressing ingredients in a blender. Process until smooth and chill.

To make salad, in a 2-quart casserole dish, layer all ingredients except chips in order listed. Spread chilled dressing over the top. Just before serving, sprinkle with crushed chips.

4 to 6 servings

Canned tuna can be substituted for the chicken.

The beauty is in the layering, so use a glass bowl or dish and resist the temptation to toss.

Salads & Such

Church Chicken Salad

Salads & Such

Great for finger sandwiches or chop chicken coarsely and use as a regular lunchtime chicken salad.

10	pounds boneless, skinless chicken	2	bunches celery, finely chopped
2	teaspoons salt or to taste	1	bunch green onions, finely chopped (optional)
1	tablespoon black pepper or to taste	1	(32-ounce) jar mayonnaise
½	teaspoon sugar	½	cup Dijon mustard

Cook chicken in a large pot of boiling water; drain. Refrigerate chicken until thoroughly chilled. Finely chop chicken in a food processor.

Mix chicken with salt, pepper and sugar. Add celery and onions and toss. Combine mayonnaise and mustard and add to chicken mixture. Blend well and chill.

Green Tomato Chutney

2	pounds green tomatoes, diced	6	cloves garlic, minced
2	pounds Granny Smith apples, diced	1½	pounds brown sugar
1	medium-size yellow onion, diced	2¼	cups cider vinegar
2	lemons, sliced into half-moons and seeded	2	tablespoons mustard seed
8	ounces raisins (about 3 cups)	1	tablespoon ground ginger
		1	teaspoon cayenne pepper
		1	teaspoon cinnamon

Combine all ingredients in a nonreactive saucepan. Cook over medium heat for 1½ hours or until mixture is thick, stirring often to prevent burning.

Pour chutney into sterilized canning jars and seal. Turn jars upside down for at least 2 minutes. Chutney is shelf stable until opened.

About 6 pints

Cranberry-Bourbon Relish

1   cup bourbon
¼   cup minced shallots
     Zest of 1 orange
1   (12-ounce) package
     fresh cranberries,
     rinsed and picked
     over

1   cup sugar
1   teaspoon freshly
     ground black pepper

Combine bourbon, shallots and orange zest in a nonreactive saucepan. Bring to a boil over medium heat. Reduce heat to a simmer and cook, stirring occasionally, for 10 minutes or until bourbon is reduced to a syrupy glaze on the bottom of the pan.

Add cranberries and sugar. Stir until sugar dissolves. Reduce heat slightly and simmer, uncovered, for 10 minutes or until most of the berries have burst open. Remove from heat and stir in pepper.

Transfer to a serving bowl. Cool to room temperature, then refrigerate until ready to serve.

Cranberry Chutney

1½   cups sliced onions
1   cup water
1½   cups dark brown sugar
1   cup granulated sugar
¾   cup cider vinegar
2   tart apples, peeled and
     diced
½   teaspoon salt
1   teaspoon grated ginger

½   teaspoon mace
½   teaspoon curry powder
     Zest and strained juice
     of 2 oranges, divided
1   pound cranberries,
     rinsed and picked
     over
½   cup currants

Combine onions, water and sugars in a stockpot. Simmer 30 minutes. Stir in vinegar, apples, salt, ginger, mace, curry powder and orange zest. Simmer 30 minutes longer.

Add orange juice, cranberries and currants. Bring to a boil. Cook until cranberries burst open. Adjust seasonings as needed. Add sugar if mixture is too sour, but avoid making chutney too sweet.

1 quart

Delicious with turkey, game or chicken...also delightful on a turkey sandwich.

30's Cranberry Sauce

Keeps for months in the refrigerator. A fine gift idea.

2 oranges, well peeled and minced
1 teaspoon cinnamon
½ teaspoon ground cloves
1 cup water

3 (12-ounce) packages fresh cranberries, rinsed and picked over
4 cups sugar
½ cup Grand Marnier liqueur
½ cup chopped walnuts

Combine oranges, cinnamon, cloves and water in a saucepan. Simmer about 10 minutes. Add cranberries and sugar. Simmer 10 minutes longer or until berries begin to pop and foam. Remove from heat.

Stir in liqueur and walnuts. Cool and refrigerate.

Suso's Pear Chutney

The extra juice may be used as a glaze for ham. Chutney is great cold or on hot Brie cheese. Also perfect served with ham and poultry.

20 cups peeled and sliced pears
2 limes, seeded and chopped
4 cloves garlic, chopped
3 large onions, chopped
5 cups raisins
3 ounces crystallized ginger, chopped, or 1 small gingerroot, chopped

2 cups chopped hot peppers
2 cups lime juice
3 cups cider vinegar
8 cups brown sugar
1 cup Worcestershire sauce

Cut pears into 1x¼-inch slices and soak in a bowl of cold water while assembling other ingredients.

Combine all other ingredients in a large pot. Cook 30 minutes. Drain pear slices and add to pot. Cook 1 hour.

Transfer chutney to sterilized canning jars and seal. Wait at least 2 weeks before serving.

Pear Chutney

10	cups diced pears	3	cups apple cider vinegar
½	cup chopped green bell pepper	½	teaspoon salt
1½	cups raisins	½	teaspoon allspice
4	cups sugar	½	teaspoon whole cloves
1	cup chopped crystallized ginger	3	cinnamon sticks

Combine pears, bell pepper, raisins, sugar, ginger, vinegar and salt in a pot.

Place allspice, cloves and cinnamon in a spice bag and tie shut. Add to pear mixture. Cook, uncovered, over low heat 1 hour or until pears are tender and sauce thickens. Remove spice bag. Transfer chutney to sterilized canning jars and seal.

Salads & Such

Fig Marmalade

3	pounds figs	2	pounds sugar
4	oranges		

Wash and dry figs well. Chop figs in a food processor and set aside. Cut oranges enough to remove seeds. Chop oranges in food processor.

Combine figs, oranges and sugar in a saucepan. Cook over low heat, stirring frequently, until mixture thickens and becomes jelly-like. Transfer to hot glass jars and seal.

Carrot Marmalade

8	large carrots (about 2 pounds)	1	cup fresh or bottled lemon juice
2	oranges, seeded and cut into chunks	7	cups sugar
		1	(6-ounce) bottle liquid pectin

Process carrots and oranges in a blender or food processor until finely chopped.

Combine carrot mixture with lemon juice and sugar in a saucepan. Cook slowly and stir for several minutes until sugar dissolves, then bring to a full boil. Boil rapidly for 1 minute, stirring constantly.

Remove from heat and stir in pectin. Stir 5 minutes to distribute solids. Skim and transfer to hot canning jars and seal.

6 (8-ounce) jars

Pickles

Colorful and compliments all meats, especially pork.

Canning was a family tradition at my grandmother's home. We called her "Granny." Aunts and cousins (women only) gathered to pop grapes for jelly or cut or shell vegetables.

8	cups sliced yellow squash	2	cups apple cider vinegar
2	cups sliced onion	1	tablespoon celery seed
3	tablespoons salt	1	tablespoon mustard seed
3½	cups sugar		

Combine squash, onion and salt and let stand 1 hour. Pack mixture into canning jars.

Mix sugar, vinegar, celery seed and mustard seed in a saucepan. Bring to a boil. Pour into prepared jars and seal.

Place jars in a large pot and cover with water. Boil for 15 minutes. Remove from water and cool at room temperature. Refrigerate jars after opening. Unopened jars will keep at least 1 year on the shelf.

Hot Pepper Jelly

1	cup chopped hot pepper	6½	cups sugar
¾	cup chopped bell pepper	1	(6-ounce) bottle liquid pectin
1½	cups white vinegar		Red or green food coloring

Combine both peppers and vinegar in a blender and chop until very fine. Transfer mixture to a saucepan and bring to a rolling boil. Stir in sugar until dissolved. Remove from heat and let stand 5 minutes. Strain, if desired.

Stir in pectin and coloring. Pour into hot, sterile canning jars. Seal with wax.

7 half-pint jars (unstrained) or 14 baby food-size jars

Using the hot pepper seed adds "heat" to the jelly. Seed peppers if milder jelly is desired.

Artichoke Pickles

½	peck (4 quarts) artichokes	2	tablespoons celery seed
1½	cups salt	2	tablespoons white mustard seed
6	cups vinegar	¼	cup salt
2½	cups sugar	1	pound onions, ground
½	tablespoon cayenne pepper		

Clean artichokes and soak with 1½ cups salt in cold water overnight.

The next day, drain artichokes, discarding salt water. Combine vinegar, sugar, pepper, celery seed, mustard seed, ¼ cup salt and onions in a saucepan. Simmer 30 minutes. Pour mixture over artichokes and let stand 24 hours.

Drain liquid into a saucepan and reheat. Pour over artichokes. Repeat two more times, letting artichokes stand 24 hours each time. Transfer artichokes and liquid to canning jars and seal.

Pickled Cabbage

*The Vestry
sent letters to
London in July
1759, asking for
a "middle-aged
man of grave
deportment,
suitable to
sacred office,
and of a good,
audible voice,
as the church is
large, to serve
as the first
rector."*

6	large heads cabbage	2	tablespoons celery seed
4	large onions	2	tablespoons dry mustard
	Salt	4	cups sugar
	Red vinegar	1	(2-ounce) jar pimento
3	tablespoons turmeric		Flour
2	tablespoons pickling spice		

Shred cabbage and onion together. Sprinkle with salt and let stand overnight.

Rinse thoroughly 3 times or until water runs clear. Squeeze out water and place in a saucepan. Add red vinegar to cover. Add turmeric, pickling spice, celery seed and mustard seed. Cook until vegetables start to soften. Stir in sugar and pimento. Add flour if needed to reach desired thickness. Cool. Transfer to canning jars and seal.

Artichoke Relish

4	pounds Jerusalem artichokes, diced	1	gallon water
2	green bell peppers, diced	½	cup flour
1	red bell pepper, diced	4	cups vinegar
2	large yellow onions, diced	5	cups sugar
1	cup canning salt	⅓	cup mustard seed
		1½	tablespoons celery seed
		1½	tablespoons turmeric

Soak artichokes, bell peppers, onions and canning salt in 1 gallon of water in refrigerator for 24 hours. Drain and rinse vegetables, removing as much water as possible.

In a large stockpot, mix flour and vinegar. Stir in sugar, mustard seed, celery seed and turmeric. Add drained vegetables. Bring to a slow boil. Transfer to sterilized canning jars and seal with lids. Turn jars upside down for 2 minutes. Relish will be shelf stable until opened.

6 pints

One of the Earliest St. Michael's Plantation Tour

For many years, St. Michael's Church, like many other historic churches, had a plantation tour to raise money for the church. The tour, which was held from 10-5 on a Saturday, was a big project, which involved many volunteers. Ladies were called on to be docents, help in food preparation, and as traffic directors. The lunch menu always consisted of okra gumbo, sandwiches and cookies.

On one of the first plantation tours lunch was to be served at Otranto Plantation on the Cooper River, which is now in a subdivision off of Rivers Avenue. Food was prepared in the kitchen while the church ladies waited for the tourist to arrive. With the lack of telephones, communication was rather poor, so these ladies never knew how many people would arrive or when. Otranto in those days was considered a long way from the city. When tourists did arrive, they quickly went upstairs to the one bathroom available. After the few flushes the toilet became very slow and the line got longer and longer.

Meanwhile, the church ladies, unaware of the long line were getting careless about the amount of food they were consuming while merrily cutting crusts off the sandwiches and tasting the soup for "seasoning." Finally a large group of tourists, mostly ladies, appeared downstairs after giving up on the slow toilet. By this time the church ladies had left very little food. Needless to say there was some shrieking in the kitchen, water poured into the soup pot to scrape up the leftover soup and regrets over cutting the crusts from the sandwiches. There was little to serve the outspoken ladies with their hats, gloves and pocketbooks in hand!

The ladies learned their lesson. The tours and food preparation became more organized long before the plumbing ever improved.

The Last St. Michael's Plantation Tour

About thirty years ago, the last St. Michael's church tour was held near Beaufort, South Carolina. The lunch was to be served at the ruins of Sheldon Church off Highway 17, north of Beaufort. Rain was in the forecast, so a few makeshift tents, including a funeral tent, were erected. Tents were not as popular or readily available as they are today. Since there were no cooking facilities, a portable gas grill was used to heat up the okra soup. The clouds were hovering over us, but no one paid attention.

Tables and chairs were set up and the most modern bathroom facilities were to arrive any moment. After a few tentative raindrops, a downpour ensued. The truck hauling the port-a-lets made a sharp turn from the highway and all the port-a-lets fell into a ditch. The driver got out and stared at the mess. With almost 500 people soon arriving for lunch there was a sense of urgency, so to speak, to get the port-a-lets upright. After much struggling, the units were still in the ditch, but upright and stable enough for those with good balance.

The rain continued as people began arriving for lunch. They were calling out of their car windows for "curb service" and were quite curious about the unusual placement of the port-a-lets.

While lunch was being served, gales of laughter came from the direction of the kitchen tent, which was beginning to leak. Water was dripping into the soup, diluting it and pools formed around the plates of sandwiches.

All in all, everyone was good-natured about the soggy sandwiches, watery soup and toilets on a slant. After the lunch, the sun began to peek out from behind the dark clouds and the day ended with wet, drippy smiles.

Breads, Brunch & Grits

"Give us this day our daily bread"

Praying Silhouette

In quiet solitude, we seek God's greatness
and mercy. Through thanksgiving, praise and repen-
tance we listen for answers. The history stained walls
within which we worship have witnessed many prayers.
The answers come in a still calm voice, sometimes
building to a roar. Maybe that's what God had
in mind with the earthquake of 1886!

"And when they had prayed, the place
was shaken where they were assembled together
and they were filled with the Holy Ghost and they
spake the word of God with boldness."
Acts 4:31

Dad's Orange Breakfast Ring

Great for Saturday morning!

1½ cups sugar
¼   cup orange zest

2   (12-ounce) cans refrigerated buttermilk biscuits
½   cup butter, melted

Icing

1   (3-ounce) package cream cheese, softened

½   cup sifted powdered sugar
2   tablespoons orange juice

Preheat oven to 350 degrees.

Combine sugar and orange zest. Dip biscuits in butter, then in sugar mixture, coating evenly. Stand biscuits on end in a greased Bundt pan to form a ring. Bake 30 minutes.

Meanwhile prepare icing by combining all ingredients until smooth.

When done baking, invert biscuit ring onto a serving plate. Spoon icing over top while hot. Serve immediately.

6 to 8 servings

Banana Bread

½   cup finely chopped pecans
1   cup sugar
1   cup self-rising flour
2   eggs
2   medium-size ripe bananas, diced or mashed

½   teaspoon cinnamon
½   teaspoon vanilla
¼   teaspoon nutmeg
4   tablespoons butter, melted

Preheat oven to 350 degrees.

Combine all ingredients and pour into a greased and floured loaf pan. Bake 50 minutes.

"I am the bread of life. Your forefathers ate the manna in the desert, yet they died. But here is the bread that comes down from heaven, which a man may eat and not die. I am the living bread that came down from heaven. If anyone eats of this bread, he will live forever. This bread is my flesh, which I will give for the life of the world."

~ John 6:48-51

Breads, Brunch & Grits

93

Cream Cheese Coffee Cake

So quick and so yummy - everyone asks for the recipe.

2	(8-count) packages crescent rolls	1	tablespoon vanilla
2	(8-ounce) packages cream cheese		Juice of ½ lemon
		1	egg white
¾	cup sugar	½	cup chopped pecans

Preheat oven to 350 degrees.

Press one package of crescent rolls into the bottom of a greased 9x13-inch pan. Press seams together.

Beat cream cheese, sugar, vanilla and lemon juice together until smooth. Spread mixture over crescent crust. Lay second package of rolls over filling, pressing seams together. Beat egg white until foamy and brush over top layer. Sprinkle pecans on top and press them in gently.

Bake 30 minutes or until golden brown. Cool before cutting to allow filling to set.

6 servings

Cinnamon Fluff Coffee Cake

½	cup shortening	1	teaspoon baking powder
⅔	cup sugar	1	teaspoon baking soda
2	eggs	½	teaspoon salt
1½	cups flour	1	cup buttermilk
2	tablespoons cinnamon		

Topping

½	cup sugar	1	tablespoon cinnamon
1	tablespoon butter		

Preheat oven to 325 degrees.

Cream shortening, sugar and eggs together. In a separate bowl, sift together flour, cinnamon, baking powder, baking soda and salt. Add dry ingredients to creamed mixture alternately with buttermilk. Pour batter into a greased and floured 9x9-inch pan.

Rub together all topping ingredients and sprinkle over batter. Bake 40 to 45 minutes.

Eulalie's Coffee Cake

½ cup butter, softened
1 cup sugar
2 eggs, slightly beaten
1½ cups self-rising
    all-purpose flour
½ cup milk
1 teaspoon vanilla

½ cup finely chopped
    pecans
1 teaspoon cinnamon, or
    more to taste
2 teaspoons sugar
¼ cup melted butter

Preheat oven to 350 degrees.

Cream butter and 1 cup sugar. Add eggs and mix until blended. Stir in flour alternately with milk. Add vanilla and mix well. Spoon batter into a greased and floured 9x11-inch baking pan.

Sprinkle pecans over batter. Combine cinnamon and 2 teaspoons sugar and sprinkle over the top. Drizzle melted butter over batter. Bake 25 to 30 minutes.

In loving memory of Mrs. Eulalie Adams Davis, for many years organist and choir director of St. Michael's Church, who baked this coffee cake and served it along with ham biscuits to the choirs on Easter morning between services.

Carrot Tea Bread

1 cup sugar
¾ cup vegetable oil
1¾ cup sifted flour
1 teaspoon baking soda
1 teaspoon baking
    powder
½ teaspoon salt

1 teaspoon cinnamon
½ teaspoon ground cloves
    or ginger (optional)
2 eggs
1 cup grated or coarsely
    ground carrot
Chopped nuts (optional)

Preheat oven to 375 degrees.

Using an electric mixer, beat sugar and oil together. Add flour, baking soda, baking powder, salt, cinnamon and cloves. Mix well. Add eggs, carrot and nuts. Beat well. Pour batter into a greased and floured loaf pan or 3 to 4 smaller loaf pans.

Bake 55 minutes for a large loaf, 40 to 45 minutes for smaller loaves or until a toothpick inserted in the center comes out clean.

1 large loaf

Banana Nut Bread

½	cup shortening	1	teaspoon baking soda
1	cup sugar	3	medium-size ripe
2	eggs, beaten		bananas, mashed
2	cups flour	½	cup chopped nuts
½	teaspoon salt		

Preheat oven to 350 degrees.

Cream shortening and sugar until smooth. Mix in eggs. In a separate bowl, sift together flour, salt and baking soda. Fold dry ingredients into creamed mixture alternately with bananas. Mix in nuts and pour batter into a greased and floured 9x5-inch loaf pan. Bake 1 hour.

8 to 10 servings

Spinach Bread

1	loaf French bread	1	(4-ounce) package
3	tablespoons butter,		grated mozzarella
	softened		cheese
1	(10-ounce) package	1	small onion, diced
	frozen chopped	¼	teaspoon garlic powder
	spinach, thawed	¼	teaspoon seasoned salt
1	egg, beaten		Parmesan cheese
1	(4-ounce) package		
	grated sharp Cheddar		
	cheese		

Preheat oven to 350 degrees.

Cut French bread in half lengthwise and spread both halves with butter. Combine spinach, egg, Cheddar cheese, mozzarella cheese, onion, garlic powder and seasoned salt. Spread mixture evenly over both halves of bread. Sprinkle with Parmesan cheese. Wrap each half tightly in foil and place on a baking sheet. Bake 15 minutes.

Open foil to expose bread. Transfer to broiler and broil at 500 degrees for 3 to 5 minutes or until top is lightly browned.

Great as an appetizer cut in small pieces.

Charles's Cornbread

1	cup self-rising cornmeal	1¼	cups sour cream
½	cup vegetable oil	1	cup cream-style corn
		2	eggs

Preheat oven to 400 degrees.

Combine all ingredients and mix well. Pour batter into a greased 8x8x2-inch baking pan. Bake 30 minutes.

12 servings

Cornbread can be frozen, but is best fresh or made a day before serving.

For a larger recipe, yielding about 48 large pieces, make a quadruple recipe (4X) and use a full sheet pan.

Ham Rolls
Good for parties and luncheons.

¾	cup butter, melted	1	medium onion, chopped
3	tablespoons prepared mustard	2	(12-count) packages dinner rolls
3	tablespoons poppy seeds	2	(6-ounce) packages smoked ham
1	tablespoon Worcestershire sauce	½	cup grated Swiss (or Cheddar) cheese

Preheat oven to 400 degrees.

Combine butter, mustard, poppy seeds, Worcestershire sauce and onion. Spoon some of butter mixture into a large baking dish.

Slice rolls in half horizontally. Place bottom half of rolls in pan. Pour about half of the remaining butter mixture over roll bottoms. Divide ham evenly among rolls. Sprinkle cheese over ham and add top of rolls. Pour remaining butter mixture over top of rolls. Bake 10 minutes.

24 servings

I have taken these rolls to several covered dish socials and they have always gone over well.

Breads, Brunch & Grits

Starbursters
Blueberry Biscuits

Yummy!! - Quick and easy.

Good at breakfast, snack time, tea or suppertime. Use a star cookie cutter. When cooked, the blueberries burst open!!

1	(8-count) can refrigerated Pillsbury Southern-style Grands biscuits (regular or low fat)		"I Can't Believe It's Not Butter" butter spray Sugar
		1	cup fresh blueberries

Preheat oven to 375 degrees.

Cut biscuits with a star cookie cutter and place on an ungreased baking sheet. Spray top of biscuits with butter spray and sprinkle with sugar. Press 7 to 10 blueberries on top of each biscuit.

Bake 11 to 15 minutes. Serve warm.

8 servings

Perfect Biscuits

"Give us today our daily bread."

~ Matthew 6:11

2	cups flour	½	teaspoon cream of tartar
½	teaspoon salt		
4	teaspoons baking powder	½	cup shortening (Crisco)
		⅔	cup milk

Preheat oven to 400 degrees.

Sift together flour, salt, baking powder and cream of tartar three or four times (a must!). Cut in shortening and add milk.

Roll out dough. Cut dough with a biscuit cutter and place biscuits on a baking sheet. Bake 10 minutes for small biscuits, 15 minutes for large biscuits.

Breads, Brunch & Grits

98

Happy's Sour Cream Biscuits

3 cups all-purpose flour	3 tablespoons shortening
5 teaspoons baking powder	2 heaping tablespoons sour cream
1 teaspoon salt	Half-and-half

Preheat oven to 450 degrees.

Combine flour, baking powder, salt, shortening and sour cream. Add enough half-and-half to moisten mixture enough to work with. Mix into a soft dough, no kneading necessary.

Roll out onto a floured board to slightly less than ½-inch thick. Fold dough over once and roll out again to the same thickness. Cut with a biscuit cutter and place on a baking sheet. Prick biscuits with a fork. Bake 12 to 15 minutes or until golden brown.

If freezing biscuits, bake only 8 to 10 minutes. Freeze in plastic bags. When ready to serve, bake at 450 degrees for 5 minutes.

3 dozen

My grandmother, Happy Booker, is a grand hostess and uses these biscuits at her many wonderful social events.

Cheese Biscuits

1 cup self-rising flour	⅛ teaspoon cayenne pepper
½ cup butter, softened	2 tablespoons milk (optional)
1 cup grated New York sharp Cheddar cheese	

Preheat oven to 375 degrees.

Combine all ingredients and mix well. Shape dough into small biscuits or roll out dough and cut with a small biscuit cutter. Place on a baking sheet. Bake about 10 minutes.

Put the bread of the Presence on this table to be before me at all times.

~ Exodus 25:30

Jean's Cheese Muffins

2	cups self-rising flour	½	teaspoon salt or less
1	cup milk	2	cups grated sharp
½	cup mayonnaise		Cheddar cheese

Preheat oven to 400 degrees.

Combine all ingredients and mix well. Bake in greased muffin tins for about 18 minutes.

10 to 14 muffins

Orange Date Muffins

2	egg yolks	1	tablespoon orange zest
1	cup brown sugar	1	cup finely chopped
½	cup all-purpose flour		dates
¼	teaspoon salt	1	cup finely chopped
½	teaspoon baking		pecans
	powder	2	egg whites
½	teaspoon vanilla		

Glaze

⅓	cup orange juice	1	tablespoon orange zest
½	cup sugar		

Preheat oven to 350 degrees.

Beat egg yolks and sugar together. Mix in flour, salt and baking powder. Add vanilla. Fold in orange zest, dates and pecans. Beat egg whites until stiff. Fold egg whites into batter. Batter will be stiff. Spoon batter into ungreased mini muffin tins, filling half-full. Bake 15 minutes.

While muffins bake, prepare glaze. Combine all glaze ingredients in a saucepan and bring to a boil. Keep hot.

Spoon 1 teaspoon glaze over each muffin immediately after removing from oven. Cool completely in muffin tins before carefully removing.

2½ to 3 dozen mini muffins

Six-Week Bran Muffins

**Great for breakfast on the run
or as welcome gifts for new neighbors.**

1	(15-ounce) box raisin bran flakes	2	teaspoons salt
1	cup brown sugar	2	teaspoons cinnamon
1	cup granulated sugar	2	teaspoons nutmeg
5	cups all-purpose flour	4	eggs, beaten
5	teaspoons baking soda	1	quart buttermilk
		1	cup vegetable oil

Combine all ingredients in a large bowl. Mix thoroughly and transfer to a covered container. Store batter in refrigerator for up to six weeks.

When ready to serve, preheat oven to 400 degrees. Bake in greased muffin tins for 12 to 15 minutes.

5 dozen

My father gave each of his daughters a huge stainless steel mixing bowl to use with this recipe. When I use mine, it "ties" me to my sister and my father in a very nice way - even though she lives in California and he has been dead over 10 years.

Dick Eichhorn's Easy "Made From Scratch" Buttermilk Pancakes

2	cups bleached flour	1	teaspoon salt
1	cup yellow cornmeal	1	egg
1	teaspoon baking powder	2	teaspoons vanilla
1	teaspoon baking soda	¼-⅓	cup vegetable oil
½	cup sugar		Buttermilk

Combine flour, cornmeal, baking powder, baking soda, sugar and salt in a large bowl. Beat egg in a measuring cup. Add vanilla, oil and some buttermilk to egg and whisk together. Pour egg mixture into dry ingredients and mix with a large spoon. Add more buttermilk as needed to reach a medium-thick consistency.

Spoon batter onto a lightly greased hot griddle. Pancakes can be made in any size, but 4- to 5-inch diameter works best. Turn when bubbles appear on top, being careful not to burn.

12 to 14 pancakes (4- to 5-inch diameter)

Fresh blueberries can be added to the batter.

Orange Upside-Down French Toast

4	tablespoons butter	4	eggs, slightly beaten
⅓	cup sugar	⅔	cup orange juice
½	teaspoon cinnamon	8	slices firm white bread
1	teaspoon orange zest		

Preheat oven to 400 degrees.

Place butter in a 15x10x1-inch pan and melt in oven.

In a small bowl, combine sugar, cinnamon and orange zest. Sprinkle evenly over butter in pan.

Combine eggs and orange juice. Dip bread slices into egg mixture, soaking each slice well. Arrange bread in a single layer in pan. Spoon any remaining egg mixture over bread. Bake about 25 minutes.

4 servings

Incredible Scrambled Eggs

3	tablespoons butter	¼	teaspoon black pepper
3	tablespoons flour	6	tablespoons butter
2	cups milk	1	(8-ounce) package
16	eggs		cream cheese
1	teaspoon salt		

To make a white sauce, melt 3 tablespoons butter in a saucepan. Stir in flour and cook until bubbling. Whisk in milk until smooth. Bring to a boil. Reduce heat and cook and stir 2 minutes. Cool slightly. Beat white sauce with eggs, salt and pepper.

Melt 6 tablespoons butter and cream cheese in a large skillet. Add egg mixture and mix well. Cook and stir until eggs start to set, but are still soft. Pour mixture into a 2-quart shallow baking dish. Cover with foil and refrigerate overnight.

When ready to serve, preheat oven to 400 degrees. Bake 10 minutes.

12 to 14 servings

St. Michael's Lenten Lunch Cheese Soufflé

12	slices day-old bread	¼	teaspoon dried mustard
2	tablespoons butter, softened	½	teaspoon Worcestershire sauce
2	cups grated sharp Cheddar cheese	¼	teaspoon cayenne pepper
8	eggs	¾	teaspoon salt
3	cups milk	¼	teaspoon black pepper

Cut off crust from bread slices. Spread slices with butter and then cut into cubes. Place bread cubes in a 9x13-inch pan. Sprinkle cheese over bread.

Beat together eggs, milk, mustard, Worcestershire sauce, cayenne pepper, salt and black pepper. Pour mixture over bread and cheese. Cover and refrigerate overnight.

When ready to serve, preheat oven to 350 degrees. Bake 1 hour.

16 servings

This recipe was a tradition during the Lenten lunch series at St. Michael's - served with salad and fresh croissants.

Molli's Breakfast Bake

6	slices white bread	1¼	cups milk
1	pound raw breakfast sausage	¾	cup half-and-half
1	tablespoon prepared mustard	1	teaspoon Worcestershire sauce
6	slices Swiss cheese		Salt and pepper to taste
5	eggs		

Arrange bread in a 9x13-inch baking dish. Brown sausage and drain fat. Mix sausage with mustard. Spoon sausage over bread. Place a slice of cheese on each bread slice.

Beat together eggs, milk, half-and-half, Worcestershire sauce, salt and pepper. Pour mixture over bread. Cover and refrigerate overnight.

When ready to serve, preheat oven to 350 degrees. Bake 30 minutes.

4 to 6 servings

Cherubic Eggs

Good finger-food item.

8   hard-cooked eggs,
   halved lengthwise
   Mayonnaise to taste

Garlic or black pepper
   to taste
Curry powder to taste
Paprika to taste

Remove egg yolks and place in a bowl. Set egg white shells aside. Mash yolks with mayonnaise, pepper and curry powder. Blend well.

Use a teaspoon to spoon yolk mixture into egg white shells. Sprinkle with paprika.

16 servings

Breads, Brunch & Grits

Spinach Egg Casserole

1   cup chopped onion
1   tablespoon butter or
   margarine
1   (10-ounce) package
   frozen chopped
   spinach, thawed
1   cup buttermilk
2   cups creamed cottage
   cheese

3   cups cooked rice
½   teaspoon salt
¼   teaspoon black pepper
4   eggs, beaten
1   large tomato, cut into
   6 slices
1   cup grated mozzarella
   cheese

Preheat oven to 350 degrees.

Sauté onion in butter until tender. Add spinach and cook about 1 minute. Remove from heat and blend in buttermilk, cottage cheese, rice, salt, pepper and eggs.

Transfer to a greased, shallow 2-quart casserole dish. Bake 25 minutes. Arrange tomato slices on top. Sprinkle with mozzarella cheese. Return to oven and bake 10 minutes longer.

6 servings

In a pinch, substitute regular milk with a dash of lemon juice for the buttermilk.

Broccoli and Sausage Quiche

1	deep dish pie crust or 2 regular pie crusts	3	eggs	
½	pound hot or mild sausage	1½	cups half-and-half	
1	(10-ounce) package frozen chopped broccoli	½	teaspoon salt	
		½	teaspoon oregano	
		⅛	teaspoon black pepper	
		1	cup grated Swiss cheese	

Preheat oven to 350 degrees.

Partially bake pie crust until just starting to brown.

Brown sausage and drain fat. Cook broccoli 3 to 5 minutes, drain and rinse with cold water. Beat together eggs, half-and-half, salt, oregano and pepper.

Spread sausage over the bottom of the pie crust. Layer half the cheese, all the broccoli and remaining cheese on top. Pour egg mixture into crust. Bake 45 minutes.

6 to 8 servings

Cast your bread upon the waters, for after many days you will find it again.

~ Ecclesiastes 11:1

Seafood Quiche

¾	pound crabmeat	½	cup minced green onions
½	pound shrimp, cooked and chopped	2	pie crusts, baked
½	pound Swiss cheese, grated	1	cup mayonnaise
½	cup minced celery	2	tablespoons flour
		1	cup dry white wine
		4	eggs, slightly beaten

Preheat oven to 350 degrees.

Combine crabmeat, shrimp, cheese, celery and onions. Spoon mixture into baked pie crusts. Combine mayonnaise, flour, wine and eggs. Pour mixture into pie crusts. Bake 35 to 40 minutes.

2 pies

Then Jesus declared, "I am the bread of life. He who comes to me will never go hungry and he who believes in me will never be thirsty."

~ John 6:35

Hominy

Hominy or Grits, as some people call it, is a corn preparation boiled with water and salt and served at the breakfast table. For many generations in the Lowcountry, hominy would be served with bacon, eggs or seafood, along with lots of butter.

It is a versatile dish that is also served for brunch or supper with ham, shrimp or crab. We mix it with cheese or gravy. It can be boiled, baked or fried, but make sure it is cooked well.

Called Hominy by Charlestonians; Grits by others, this is a dish that has been enjoyed for many, many years.

Spinach-Onion Quiche Squares

Great for breakfast!

Crust

1¾	cups all-purpose flour	¾	cup butter, slightly softened

Filling

1	medium onion, diced	1	(12-ounce) can evaporated skim milk
1	tablespoon butter	3	eggs
1	(10-ounce) package frozen spinach, cooked and well drained	¼	teaspoon salt
		⅛	teaspoon black pepper
		⅛	teaspoon nutmeg
1	cup grated Swiss cheese		

Preheat oven to 375 degrees.

Place flour and butter in an 8x12-inch pan. Cut butter coarsely into flour with a pastry blender or fork. Press mixture into bottom of pan with a tablespoon. Bake 10 minutes. Cool slightly.

To make filling, sauté onion in butter and sprinkle over baked crust. Sprinkle spinach and cheese on top. Beat together milk, eggs, salt, pepper and nutmeg. Pour mixture over crust. Bake 20 to 25 minutes.

8 to 10 servings

South Carolina Grits

1	cup milk	¼	teaspoon white pepper
1	cup chicken broth	½	cup grits
1	teaspoon salt		

Bring milk, broth, salt and pepper to a boil. Add grits. Reduce heat to medium. Cover and simmer 20 minutes, stirring occasionally.

6 servings

Janet's Grits Casserole

4 cups water
1 cup grits
½ cup margarine
1 cup grated Cheddar or
   American cheese

Salt to taste
Grated onion to taste
2 eggs
   Milk

This is almost like a soufflé and is a nice starch instead of potatoes or rice.

Preheat oven to 350 degrees.

Bring water to a boil. Stir in grits and cook until tender and the consistency of pudding. Add margarine, cheese, salt and onion.

Place eggs in a 1-cup measuring cup and beat until mixed. Add milk to total 1 cup volume. Add egg mixture to cooked grits and mix thoroughly. Transfer to a greased square casserole dish. Bake, uncovered, 1 hour.

Hominy Surprise

8 cups water
2 cups regular or stone-
   ground grits
1 tablespoon salt
2 eggs, beaten
1 cup grated sharp
   Cheddar cheese

1 tablespoon black
   pepper or to taste
1 tablespoon
   Worcestershire sauce
1 cup milk
½ cup butter
½ cup grated cheese
   Paprika

This is especially good with sliced ham, sausage or bacon and eggs for breakfast.

Bring water to a boil. Add grits and salt and cook 30 to 40 minutes, stirring frequently. (Reduce cooking time if using quick grits.)

Add eggs, 1 cup Cheddar cheese, pepper, Worcestershire sauce, milk and butter to grits. Mix thoroughly and transfer to a baking dish. Top with ½ cup grated cheese and sprinkle with paprika.

When ready to serve, preheat oven to 350 degrees. Bake about 45 minutes.

8 servings

Breads, Brunch & Grits

Tortilla Chiles Rellenos Casserole

8	corn tortillas	1	pound Monterey Jack
	Vegetable oil		or Pepper Jack
4	(4.5-ounce) cans whole		cheese, grated
	or chopped green	6	eggs
	chiles	2	cups low-fat milk
3	tomatoes, sliced	1-2	teaspoons cumin
		1	teaspoon salt

Preheat oven to 350 degrees.

Fry tortillas briefly in oil and drain on paper towels. Break tortillas into pieces to fit into a 9x13-inch baking dish. Layer half of each of the tortilla pieces, chiles, tomato slices and cheese in dish. Repeat layers.

Beat together eggs, milk, cumin and salt until frothy. Pour all or enough to reach top layers over casserole. Bake 30 minutes. Remove from oven and let stand 15 minutes before serving.

6 to 8 servings

Chiles Rellenos Torte

1	pound Monterey Jack	2	(4½-ounce) cans whole
	cheese, grated		or chopped green
1	pound sharp Cheddar		chiles
	cheese, grated	6	small tomatoes,
4	eggs, separated		chopped, or
1	(5-ounce) can		1 (14½-ounce) can
	evaporated milk		Italian tomatoes,
2	tablespoons flour		drained

Preheat oven to 325 degrees.

Mix together cheeses. Combine egg yolks, milk and flour in a bowl. In a separate bowl, beat egg whites until stiff. Fold whites into yolk mixture.

In a greased casserole dish, layer half of each of the chiles, cheese mixture and egg mixture. Repeat layers. Bake 30 minutes.

Remove from oven and top with tomatoes. Bake 30 minutes longer if tomatoes are fresh, 10 minutes for canned tomatoes. Casserole is done when it is firm and set and a knife inserted in the center comes out clean.

6 to 8 servings

Vegetables & Grains

"Chaffing the wheat"

Christmas Altar

After the penitential season of Advent,
we cannot wait to adorn the Altar at St Michael's
which glows with the magic of the long awaited birth
of the Christ child. Poinsettias bursting with color
and evergreens symbolizing new life surround the altar.
Communicants kneel at a wrought iron rail dating
from 1772, which was imported from England. The
magnificent Tiffany window radiates with the image
of our patron St. Michael and draws one's
focus to the Sanctuary.

"For unto you is born this day in the city
of David a savior which is Christ the Lord."
Luke 2:11

Easy Hollandaise Sauce

2	egg yolks	⅛	teaspoon white pepper
1	tablespoon lemon juice	½	cup hot melted butter
⅛	teaspoon salt		

Combine egg yolks, lemon juice, salt and pepper in a blender. With motor running, slowly pour hot butter into blender. Spoon sauce over vegetables.

1 cup

Sweet and Sour Green Beans

Delicious with a pork roast and sweet potatoes.

1½-2	pounds fresh green beans	1	teaspoon dry mustard
1	quart water	1½	teaspoons salt
	Salt to taste	¼	cup brown sugar
6	slices bacon	2	tablespoons granulated sugar
2	medium onions, thinly sliced	¼	cup apple cider or white vinegar

Wash beans and snap into 2-inch pieces. Combine beans, 1 quart water and salt to taste in a saucepan and bring to a boil. Reduce heat and simmer 10 to 15 minutes. Drain, reserving 1 cup liquid. Set aside beans and liquid.

Cook bacon in saucepan until crisp. Remove bacon and crumble, reserving fat in pan. Add onions to pan and sauté. Gradually stir in mustard.

Combine salt and sugars in a separate bowl. Stir in reserved bean liquid and vinegar. Pour mixture over onions. Bring to a boil, stirring to blend. Add beans and bacon. Cover and simmer 15 minutes.

4 to 6 servings

Vegetables & Grains

Herb Green Beans

2	(15-ounce) cans "Blue Lake" green beans, drained	½	teaspoon dried parsley
3	tablespoons margarine	¼	teaspoon Accent seasoning
1	stalk celery, finely chopped	¼	teaspoon dried rosemary
½	teaspoon minced garlic	¼	teaspoon dried tarragon

Preheat oven to 325 degrees.

Arrange beans in a casserole dish. Melt margarine in a small saucepan. Add celery, garlic, parsley, Accent, rosemary and tarragon. Sauté 3 to 5 minutes. Drizzle mixture over beans.

Bake, uncovered, for 15 to 20 minutes. Serve immediately.

5 servings

Stuffing Pie

4	tablespoons butter	2	cups cubed day old bread
2	pounds sausage	2	cups dry herbed stuffing mix
6	stalks celery, finely chopped	½	cup chicken broth
2	large onions, finely chopped	¼	cup heavy cream
1	clove garlic, minced	¼	cup chopped fresh sage
2	pounds fresh spinach, washed and chopped		Salt and pepper to taste

Preheat oven to 350 degrees.

Crumble sausage into a skillet and brown over medium heat. Drain and set aside sausage in a large bowl, reserving fat in skillet. Add celery, onions and garlic to skillet and sauté until softened. Add spinach and cook 1 to 2 minutes longer. Add spinach mixture to sausage. Fold in bread cubes, stuffing mix, broth, cream, sage, salt and pepper. Mix thoroughly.

Press mixture into 2 greased 10-inch glass pie pans or a 9x13-inch baking dish. Bake, uncovered, 45 minutes. Top will brown and bottom will form a dark crust. Cool 20 minutes. Cut and serve.

12 servings

Carrots with Curry and Cilantro

3	tablespoons butter	1	pound medium carrots, diagonally sliced ¼-inch thick
1	teaspoon minced fresh ginger		Salt and pepper to taste
1	clove garlic, minced		
¾	teaspoon curry powder	3	tablespoons chopped fresh cilantro
¼	cup canned low-salt chicken broth		
2	tablespoons apricot preserves		

Melt butter in a skillet over medium heat. Add ginger, garlic and curry and sauté 30 seconds. Stir in broth and preserves. Add carrots, cover and simmer 6 minutes or until crisp-tender and coated with sauce.

Season with salt and pepper. Mix in cilantro.

6 servings

Quick and Easy Asparagus Casserole

1	(12-ounce) can asparagus spears	¼	cup mayonnaise
2	egg whites, beaten stiff	½	cup grated extra sharp Cheddar cheese
3	tablespoons finely minced onion	1	(2-ounce) jar diced pimento, drained

Preheat oven to 325 to 350 degrees.

Cut tips from asparagus spears and reserve for garnish. Place asparagus spears in a casserole dish coated with cooking spray.

In a mixing bowl, fold together egg whites, onion and mayonnaise. Spread mixture over asparagus. Sprinkle with cheese and top with pimento and reserved asparagus tips. Bake 20 minutes or until egg whites are set.

2 to 3 servings

Mom's Sweet Corn Pudding

½ cup sugar
2 tablespoons flour
1 teaspoon salt
3 eggs

2 cups milk
2 cups fresh or canned
    corn
    Butter

Preheat oven to 375 degrees.

Combine sugar, flour and salt. Slowly beat in eggs and milk. Add corn and mix well. Pour into a greased round glass dish. Dot with butter. Bake 45 to 50 minutes or until firm.

8 to 10 servings

Godmother's Spinach Madeline

3 (10-ounce) packages
    frozen chopped
    spinach
4 tablespoons butter
2 tablespoons chopped
    onion
2 tablespoons flour
½ cup evaporated milk
½ teaspoon black pepper
¾ teaspoon onion salt

½ teaspoon salt
1 teaspoon
    Worcestershire sauce
    Cayenne pepper to
    taste
1 (6-ounce) roll jalapeño
    cheese, cut into
    chunks
    Saltine or butter
    cracker crumbs

Preheat oven to 350 degrees.

Cook spinach as directed on package. Drain, reserving ½ cup of liquid.

Melt butter in a saucepan. Add onions and sauté until softened. Blend in flour. Add milk and reserved cooking liquid and cook and stir over low heat until smooth. Add black pepper, onion salt, salt, Worcestershire sauce, cayenne pepper and cheese. Stir until melted and smooth.

Pour mixture into a greased casserole dish. Top with crumbs. Place casserole dish in a pan of water in the oven. Bake 1 hour.

8 servings

Stuffed Tomatoes

3	large tomatoes	¼	cup sliced almonds
5	tablespoons margarine, softened	½	cup mayonnaise
½	cup dry seasoned bread crumbs	2	tablespoons sour cream
¼	cup Parmesan cheese	1	teaspoon minced fresh dill

Preheat oven to 375 degrees.

Cut tops off of tomatoes and core partially.

Combine margarine, bread crumbs, cheese and almonds to make a stuffing. This can easily be done in a food processor.

In a separate bowl, mix together mayonnaise, sour cream and dill.

Spoon stuffing into tomatoes. Bake 30 minutes. Top with sour cream mixture before serving.

3 servings

The original Rector's salary was about 112 pounds sterling and a comfortable house.

Squash Zucchini Casserole

4-5	yellow crookneck summer squash, sliced ¼-inch thick	2	eggs, beaten
2	zucchini, sliced ¼-inch thick	4	tablespoons butter or margarine
1	onion, chopped		Salt and pepper to taste
		½	cup grated Cheddar cheese

Preheat oven to 350 degrees.

Boil squash, zucchini and onion in lightly salted water for 15 minutes or until tender. Drain well and place in a large casserole dish. Add eggs and butter while vegetables are hot. Mix well. Season with salt and pepper to taste. Sprinkle cheese evenly over top.

Bake 5 minutes. Cover and bake 25 to 30 minutes longer, removing cover for last 5 minutes of baking time.

12 servings

Vegetables & Grains

Spinach Pie

3	cups chopped yellow onion	½	cup pine nuts
2	tablespoons virgin olive oil	8	ounces feta cheese
2	teaspoons kosher or other coarse salt	½	cup freshly grated Parmesan cheese
1½	teaspoons freshly ground black pepper	3	tablespoons plain dry bread crumbs
3	(10-ounce) packages frozen chopped spinach, thawed and squeezed dry	6	extra large eggs, beaten
		2	teaspoons nutmeg
		6	sheets phyllo dough, thawed
		½	cup butter, melted

Preheat oven to 350 degrees.

Sauté onion in oil until translucent and slightly browned. Stir in salt and pepper and cool.

Place spinach in a bowl. Gently mix in nuts, cheeses, bread crumbs, eggs, nutmeg and sautéed onion.

Line a greased, nonstick 9-inch pie plate or casserole dish with phyllo sheets, brushing each sheet with melted butter as it is placed in dish. Pour spinach mixture into dish. Fold hanging edges of phyllo over spinach mixture and seal. Brush top well with melted butter. Bake 1 hour or until top is golden brown and filling is set.

8 servings

Confetti Bean Bake

1	(16-ounce) can black beans, drained	1	(16-ounce) can Great Northern beans, drained
1	(16-ounce) can lima beans, drained	4	tablespoons butter
1	(16-ounce) can kidney beans, drained	1	teaspoon dry mustard
		½	teaspoon salt
		2½	teaspoons molasses
		1	cup sour cream

Preheat oven to 350 degrees.

Combine all ingredients and place in a greased baking dish. Bake 45 minutes.

10 servings

Cheddar Squash Bake

2 pounds yellow crookneck summer squash, sliced
Salt
1 cup sour cream
2 eggs, separated
2 tablespoons flour
1½ cups grated Cheddar cheese

4 slices bacon, cooked crisp, drained and crumbled
⅓ cup fine dry bread crumbs
1 tablespoon butter, melted
Parsley for garnish (optional)

Don't prepare this on a hot day in a hot kitchen!

Preheat oven to 350 degrees.

Cook squash until tender; drain well. Sprinkle squash lightly with salt.

In a mixing bowl, mix sour cream, egg yolks and flour. Beat egg whites until stiff and fold into sour cream mixture.

In a 13x9-inch baking dish, layer half the squash, half the egg mixture and half the cheese. Repeat layers. Sprinkle with bacon. Combine bread crumbs and butter and sprinkle over top. Bake 20 to 25 minutes. Garnish with parsley.

8 servings

Eggplant Pie

2 medium eggplant, peeled and cubed	¼-½ teaspoon ground thyme
1 medium onion, chopped	Salt and pepper to taste
½ tablespoon butter	2-3 tablespoons butter, softened
2 eggs, divided	½ cup grated sharp Cheddar cheese
¼-½ cup milk	½ cup saltine cracker crumbs
½ cup grated sharp Cheddar cheese	

Preheat oven to 350 degrees.

Cook eggplant in boiling water until softened. Drain well. Meanwhile, sauté onion in ½ tablespoon butter until softened.

Combine half the eggplant, half the onion, 1 egg and enough milk to cover in a blender. Puree. Repeat with remaining eggplant, onion and egg and milk to cover. Combine pureed mixtures in a mixing bowl. While still hot, stir in ½ cup cheese, thyme, salt and pepper. Mix well. Add 2 to 3 tablespoons butter and stir until melted.

Pour mixture into a 2-quart casserole dish. Bake, uncovered, for 20 to 30 minutes. Sprinkle ½ cup cheese and cracker crumbs on top. Bake 8 minutes longer.

6 to 7 servings

Janet's Fried Green Tomatoes

2 green tomatoes	1 egg
¼ teaspoon salt	¼ cup heavy cream
¼ teaspoon black pepper	2 cups cornmeal
1 cup flour	Vegetable oil

Slice tomatoes into ½-inch thick slices. Mix salt, pepper and flour in a shallow dish. In a mixing bowl, beat egg. Mix in cream. Dip tomato slices in flour mixture, then into egg mixture, then dredge in cornmeal. Refrigerate 15 to 30 minutes.

Add oil to an iron skillet to 2 inches deep. Heat to about 325 degrees. Add tomato slices and fry 3 minutes or until golden brown.

4 servings

Broccoli Stuffed Onions

3 medium to large
Vidalia onions, peeled
and halved
1 (10-ounce) package
frozen chopped
broccoli
½ cup Parmesan cheese
⅓ cup mayonnaise (not
salad dressing type)

2 teaspoons lemon juice
2 tablespoons butter
2 tablespoons flour
¼ teaspoon salt
⅔ cup milk
1 (3-ounce) package
cream cheese, cubed

Frozen, chopped spinach can be used in place of broccoli.

Preheat oven to 375 degrees.

Parboil onion halves in salted water for 10 to 12 minutes; drain. Remove onion centers, leaving a ¾-inch shell. Chop center portions to equal 1 cup. Cool. Cook broccoli as directed on package. Drain and cool.

Combine chopped onion, broccoli, Parmesan cheese, mayonnaise and lemon juice. Spoon mixture into onion shells and place in a baking dish.

Melt butter in a saucepan. Blend in flour and salt. Add milk and cook and stir until thickened. Remove from heat and blend in cream cheese. Spoon sauce over onions. Bake, uncovered, for 20 minutes.

6 servings

Tomato Casserole

2 (28-ounce) cans peeled
tomatoes, or 24 fresh,
peeled
⅓ cup dark brown sugar

Salt and pepper to taste
1 cup bread crumbs
3 tablespoons butter or
margarine

Excellent for picnics and dinner parties.

Preheat oven to 350 degrees.

Cut tomatoes into strips, discarding juice and seeds. Place half the tomato strips in a greased baking dish. Sprinkle generously with sugar and season with salt and pepper.

Top with a layer of bread crumbs. Dot with butter. Repeat layers. Bake 30 to 35 minutes.

8 servings

Waddy Thompson's Broccoli Casserole

Waddy Thompson was a professor at Carlisle Military Academy in Bamberg, SC. On weekends, the cadets who couldn't go home would pile into Waddy's house. This is one of the recipes used to feed a houseful of hungry, growing teenage boys.

2	(10-ounce) packages frozen chopped broccoli	1	cup mayonnaise
½	cup butter	2	eggs
½	cup chopped onion	1	cup butter cracker crumbs
2	stalks celery, chopped	2	(4-ounce) cans mushrooms, drained
1	clove garlic, chopped		Salt and pepper to taste
1	cup condensed cream of mushroom soup	1	cup butter cracker crumbs
1½	cups grated sharp Cheddar cheese		

Preheat oven to 350 degrees.

Cook broccoli as directed on package. Drain and place in a large bowl.

Melt butter in a skillet. Add onion, celery and garlic and sauté. Add mixture to broccoli. Stir in soup, cheese, mayonnaise, eggs, 1 cup cracker crumbs and mushrooms. Season with salt and pepper.

Pour mixture into a greased casserole dish. Top with 1 cup cracker crumbs. Bake 30 minutes.

8 servings

Eggplant Sauce Mornay

Great with beef!

2	eggplants, sliced	5	tablespoons flour
6	tomatoes, sliced	2	cups milk
	Vegetable oil	½-¾	cup grated Gruyère cheese
4	tablespoons butter		

Preheat oven to 350 degrees.

Brown eggplant and tomato slices in oil. Drain and layer in a baking dish.

Melt butter in a skillet. Blend in flour and cook but do not brown. Slowly add milk and stir quickly until smooth. Cook over medium heat for a few minutes. Remove from heat and stir in cheese. Pour sauce over eggplant and tomato slices. Bake 15 minutes.

6 servings

Wadmalaw Sweet Onion Bake

3-4 large Wadmalaw
    (or Vidalia) sweet
    onions, sliced
½ cup butter
1 pound Swiss cheese,
    grated

1 (10¾-ounce) can
    condensed cream of
    mushroom or cream
    of chicken soup
½ cup milk
    Salt and pepper to taste
3-4 slices bread, buttered
    and cut into 1-inch
    squares

Preheat oven to 350 degrees.

Sauté onions in butter until translucent. Transfer to a greased baking dish. Sprinkle cheese on top.

Combine soup, milk, salt and pepper and pour over onion mixture. Top with bread squares. Bake 30 to 45 minutes or until lightly browned on top.

4 to 6 servings

John's Island Tomato Pie

1 (9-inch) deep-dish pie
    crust, unbaked
5 large tomatoes, cored
    and thickly sliced
¾ teaspoon basil
    Salt and pepper to
    taste
1 onion, sliced

¾ cup mayonnaise
¼ cup grated sharp
    Cheddar cheese
1 dash hot pepper sauce
1-2 teaspoons
    Worcestershire sauce
¼ cup grated Cheddar
    cheese

Preheat oven to 375 degrees.

Bake pie crust 8 to 10 minutes. Arrange some tomato slices in pie crust. Sprinkle with basil, salt and pepper. Place some onion slices over tomatoes. Repeat tomato, onion and seasoning layers until used up.

Combine mayonnaise, ¼ cup Cheddar cheese, pepper sauce and Worcestershire sauce. Pour mixture over tomatoes and onion. Cover with ¼ cup cheese.

Bake at 400 degrees for 35 minutes or until brown. Let stand 3 to 4 minutes before cutting.

8 servings

Vegetables & Grains

Tonnie's Broccoli Casserole

Easy and delicious and gets better as a leftover.

2 (10-ounce) packages frozen chopped broccoli
1 (10¾-ounce) can condensed cream of celery soup
1 cup mayonnaise
2 eggs, beaten

2 tablespoons chopped onion
1 cup grated sharp Cheddar cheese
Salt and pepper to taste
Cheese cracker crumbs for topping

Combine all ingredients except cracker crumbs. Transfer to a baking dish, cover and refrigerate overnight.

When ready to serve, preheat oven to 400 degrees. Top casserole with cracker crumbs. Bake 30 minutes.

6 servings

Sweet Potato Soufflé

Fabulous at Thanksgiving

3 cups cooked and mashed sweet potatoes
1 cup granulated sugar
2 eggs, beaten
½ cup butter, melted
1 teaspoon vanilla

½ cup milk
1 cup brown sugar
⅓ cup flour
1 cup chopped pecans
4 tablespoons butter, melted

Preheat oven to 350 degrees.

Combine potatoes, granulated sugar, eggs, ½ cup butter, vanilla and milk. Pour mixture into a greased casserole dish.

Mix brown sugar, flour, pecans and 4 tablespoons butter and pour over potato mixture. Bake 35 minutes.

10 servings

Vegetables & Grains

Sizemore Potatoes

5	pounds russet potatoes	2	cups butter
2	large onions, chopped		(not margarine)
2	large green bell		Salt and pepper to
	peppers, chopped, or		taste
	1 (16-ounce) package		
	frozen		

Cook unpeeled potatoes in boiling water until not quite done. Peel and cut into large chunks.

Sauté onion and bell pepper in butter in a large, heavy pot until softened but not browned. Add potatoes and season with salt and pepper. Cook over very low heat, stirring often. Cook as long as possible, the longer the better.

8 to 12 servings

These are called Sizemore Potatoes because the man who always cooked at my father's barbecue was named Sizemore. At the family farm, he always cooked these in a big, black wash pot (I'm sure it was only used for cooking.)

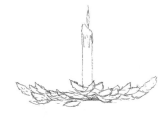

Cindy's Christmas Cheese Potatoes

6	large potatoes	¼-½	cup chopped green
2	cups coarsely grated		onion
	Cheddar cheese	1	teaspoon salt
4	tablespoons butter	¼	teaspoon black pepper
2	cups sour cream	2	tablespoons butter

Bake potatoes in skin. Cool and peel.

Preheat oven to 350 degrees. In a skillet over low heat, stir together cheese and 4 tablespoons butter until almost melted. Remove from heat and blend in sour cream, onion, salt and pepper. Gently fold in potatoes.

Use 2 tablespoons butter to grease a 2-quart casserole dish. Spoon potato mixture into dish. Bake 25 minutes.

6 to 8 servings

My sister-in-law incorporates these into her Christmas dinner when she serves tenderloin.

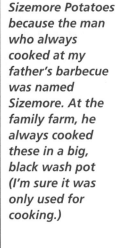

Vegetables & Grains

Lucius Beebe's St. Michael's Baked Potatoes

My husband enjoys preparing these for St. Michael's Food Fairs or for gifts to friends.

10	large baking potatoes	1	teaspoon freshly ground black pepper
1	cup butter		
8	ounces sharp Cheddar cheese, grated	2	tablespoons dried chives
		8	ounces bacon, cooked crisp and crumbled
2	teaspoons salt		

Preheat oven to 450 degrees.

Wash potatoes and prick with a fork. Bake for about 1 hour. Cut off a thin slice from top of each potato and scoop out pulp, leaving shell intact and reserving pulp.

While still hot, place pulp in a mixing bowl. Add butter, cheese, salt, pepper, chives and bacon. Mix well and stuff into potato shells. Serve immediately, or wrap in foil and freeze. Reheat frozen potatoes in a 450 degree oven or unwrapped in a microwave oven on high for 5 minutes.

10 servings

Mary Larsen's Sweet Potatoes

1	(40-ounce) can yams, drained and mashed	4	tablespoons butter, melted
½	cup sugar	½	cup milk
½	teaspoon salt	½	teaspoon vanilla
2	eggs, beaten		

Topping

1	cup brown sugar	4	tablespoons butter, melted
⅓	cup flour		
1	cup chopped pecans		

Preheat oven to 350 degrees.

Combine all ingredients except topping ingredients. Mix well and pour into a greased casserole dish.

Combine all topping ingredients and sprinkle over sweet potatoes. Bake 35 minutes.

6 to 8 servings

Okra Pilau

6   slices bacon, chopped
1   pound okra, sliced
1½ cups dry long grain rice
1¼ cups water
    Salt and pepper to
    taste

Fry bacon until half cooked. Add okra and cook 5 minutes. Stir in rice, water, salt and pepper. Pour mixture into a rice steamer. Cook 1 to 1½ hours or until rice just starts to dry.

6 servings

Green Rice

6   tablespoons butter
1   cup chopped onion
2   cups chopped celery
2   cups cooked white rice
    Salt and pepper to taste
    Dash of oregano
1   cup chopped fresh
    parsley

Melt butter in a large sauté pan. Add onion and celery and sauté until tender. Add rice, salt, pepper and oregano. Cook and stir constantly until slightly browned. Add parsley and blend well.

4 servings

Brown Rice

1   medium onion, chopped
1   bell pepper, chopped
1   stalk celery, chopped
4   tablespoons margarine
1   (10½-ounce) can beef
    consommé
1   (10¾-ounce) can
    condensed cream of
    mushroom soup
1   cup dry rice

Preheat oven to 350 degrees.

Sauté onion, bell pepper and celery in margarine in an ovenproof pan. Mix in consommé and soup. Stir in rice. Cover and bake 1½ hours.

4 to 6 servings

This is my mother's recipe and the only way I ever like okra (except for pickled okra).

Carolina Gold Rice

Charleston's greatest economic growth in the early Colonial days was due to the development of the rice culture. The first seed was brought to the province of Carolina about 1685, and became a successful export crop for about two centuries. It was called Carolina Gold Rice because of the economic wealth it brought to the Lowcountry.

To this day, many Lowcountry families consider rice as a daily must for meals. There are many recipes that have been in use for many years passing from one generation to another.

Whether brown, white, red, or green; fried or boiled, for many Charlestonians, a meal is not a meal without a good rice dish. A local favorite is Red Rice (see next page).

Vegetables & Grains

Red Rice

What would the South be without its Red Rice? A staple at every summer picnic.

8	slices bacon, cubed	2	(tomato paste) cans water
1	large sweet onion, chopped	1	tablespoon salt
½	green bell pepper, chopped	1	tablespoon sugar
1	(6-ounce) can tomato paste	2	dashes Tabasco sauce
		¼	teaspoon black pepper
		2	cups dry long-grain rice

Cook bacon in a skillet. Remove bacon, drain and set aside, reserving fat in skillet. Add onion to skillet and sauté until translucent. Add bell pepper and cook 10 minutes. Stir in tomato paste, water, salt, sugar, Tabasco sauce and black pepper. Cook, uncovered, about 10 to 15 minutes.

Stir in rice and transfer to the top of a rice steamer. Cook 1 hour to 1 hour, 15 minutes, stirring in bacon halfway through cooking time.

6 servings

Low-Fat Red Rice

2	large onions, chopped	2	tablespoons olive oil
2	stalks celery, chopped	1	(8-ounce) can Italian-style tomato sauce
1	(14- to 16-ounce) package fat-free or low-fat sausage, sliced ⅛-inch thick	2	cups dry rice
		2	tablespoons sugar
			Salt and pepper to taste

Sauté onions, celery and sausage in olive oil until onions are softened. Combine tomato sauce with enough water to equal 2 cups in volume. Stir into sausage mixture and simmer 2 minutes.

Stir in rice and simmer 2 minutes. Add sugar, salt and pepper. Pour mixture into the top of a rice steamer. Cook 1 hour.

8 servings

Easy Spicy Light Beans and Rice

2 cups dry quick-cooking brown rice
2 (15-ounce) cans beans, preferably low-sodium kidney or pinto beans
½-1 cup salsa or to taste (mild, medium or hot also to taste)
1-2 cloves garlic, minced
½ large red onion, chopped
2 teaspoons cumin
2-3 cups tomato sauce
8 dashes Tabasco sauce (optional)

Cook rice according to package directions. Rinse beans in a colander.

In a large nonstick skillet, combine salsa, garlic, onion and cumin and cook over medium-high heat until onion is softened. Add beans, tomato sauce and Tabasco sauce. Gently stir together. Simmer until well heated. Serve over cooked rice.

4 (1-cup) servings

The Best Macaroni Pie

1 (8-ounce) package elbow macaroni
4 eggs
1 cup half-and-half
1 teaspoon dry mustard
1 tablespoon Worcestershire sauce
2 cups grated sharp or extra sharp Cheddar cheese
4 tablespoons butter or margarine

Preheat oven to 350 degrees.

Cook macaroni according to package directions; drain and set aside.

Beat eggs, half-and-half, mustard and Worcestershire sauce together. Stir in macaroni and cheese.

Transfer to a greased 8-inch square casserole dish. Dot with butter. Bake 30 minutes or until bubbly.

6 servings

Pasta Fagioli (Beans)

"Quick meal"

This is a quick pasta dish my mother's mother, Filomena Capuano Gatto, would make when in a hurry.

3	cloves garlic, minced	1	(16-ounce) can cannellini beans, undrained
4	teaspoons olive oil		
1	(28-ounce) can crushed tomatoes	1	(16-ounce) package ditalini or elbow pasta
1	teaspoon oregano		Parmesan cheese to taste
	Salt and pepper to taste		

Sauté garlic in oil. Add tomatoes, oregano, salt and pepper and simmer 5 to 7 minutes. Add beans and continue to simmer 5 minutes.

Meanwhile, cook pasta according to package directions. Drain, reserving 1 cup of cooking liquid. Add pasta and reserved cooking liquid to bean mixture. Simmer 5 to 10 minutes.

Serve in bowls with cheese sprinkled on top.

4 servings

Baked Stuffed Shells

These were a holiday special - my grandfather, Emilio Gatto, would prepare the sauce and I would stuff the shells.

3-4	cups marinara sauce	2	tablespoons parsley
2	pounds ricotta cheese	1	egg
3	tablespoons Parmesan or Romano cheese	1	(12-ounce) package jumbo shells

Preheat oven to 350 degrees.

Heat marinara in a saucepan. Place a heaping cup of sauce in a large casserole dish or roasting pan.

Combine cheeses, parsley and egg. Cook pasta shells according to package directions; drain.

Spoon cheese mixture into drained shells and arrange in a single layer in dish. Bake 15 to 20 minutes. Serve with remaining hot marinara sauce.

5 to 6 servings

Vegetables & Grains

Spinach Pizza

5-6	tablespoons olive oil	4	ounces fresh mushrooms, sliced
1	(16-ounce) pre-baked pizza crust	1	tomato, thinly sliced (optional)
1	(10-ounce) package fresh spinach, cleaned and stemmed	2-3	tablespoons crumbled feta cheese (optional)
3	cloves garlic	4	ounces provolone cheese, thinly sliced
¼-½	teaspoon cayenne pepper	3	tablespoons Parmesan cheese
¼-½	teaspoon salt		

Preheat oven to 425 degrees.

Drizzle a pizza pan with some of olive oil. Place crust on pan.

Finely chop spinach and garlic in a food processor. Combine spinach mixture with cayenne pepper, salt and remainder of olive oil. Spread mixture over pizza crust.

Top with mushrooms, tomato and feta. Arrange provolone on top and sprinkle with Parmesan cheese. Bake 15 to 20 minutes or until provolone melts and is slightly browned. Let stand 5 minutes before slicing.

4 servings

This is a recipe that my husband created and would make for me when we were dating. Originally, the crust was made from homemade pizza dough. Now that we are busy with 2 young children, this is our favorite quick dinner.

Vegetables & Grains

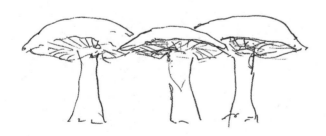

Fettuccini Florentine

1	pound ground turkey	1	(8-ounce) package Neufchâtel cheese
½	cup chopped onion	½	cup low-fat sour cream
2	cloves garlic, minced	⅓	cup chopped green onion
1	tablespoon olive oil	½	green bell pepper, chopped
1	(28-ounce) can crushed tomatoes	½-1	(10-ounce) package frozen chopped spinach
1	teaspoon sugar	1	(8-ounce) package fettuccini
¾	teaspoon salt	¼	cup Parmesan cheese
¼	teaspoon black pepper		
¼-½	teaspoon oregano		
¼-½	teaspoon basil		
8	ounces firm tofu, crumbled		

Preheat oven to 350 degrees.

Cook turkey, onion and garlic in olive oil until onions are slightly browned and tender. Add tomatoes, sugar, salt, black pepper, oregano and basil and simmer.

Mix tofu, Neufchâtel cheese, sour cream, green onion and bell pepper in a bowl. Cook spinach and fettuccini, separately, according to package directions. Drain both.

Spread a small amount of meat sauce in the bottom of a greased 9x13-inch lasagna or baking pan. Add layers of drained fettuccini and spinach. Add remainder of meat sauce. Spoon tofu mixture on top and partially swirl it into the meat sauce. Sprinkle with Parmesan cheese. Bake 30 minutes.

6 to 8 servings

Spinach Lasagna

"Always a favorite"

1	(16-ounce) package lasagna noodles Marinara sauce
1	pound ricotta cheese
3	(10-ounce) packages frozen chopped spinach

8 ounces mozzarella cheese, thinly sliced or grated

1½ cups Parmesan cheese
Black pepper to taste

Preheat oven to 350 degrees.

Prepare noodles according to package directions; drain.

Ladle just enough marinara sauce into a 9x13-inch lasagna or baking dish to make a thin layer over bottom of pan. Make a single layer of noodles over sauce. Add another thin layer of sauce. Top with a layer of ricotta cheese and a layer of spinach. Sprinkle with mozzarella and then Parmesan cheese.

Repeat layers, starting with sauce and ending with mozzarella and Parmesan cheese. Season each layer with pepper. Bake 40 minutes.

Cooked ground round or Italian sausage can be used instead of spinach.

4 to 6 servings

Spaghetti Aglio e Olio (Garlic and Oil)

Quick main dish

The scent of garlic throughout the home is wonderful. My mother would have us thinking she was preparing one of many elaborate dishes.

1	(16-ounce) package spaghetti	½	cup olive oil
2	teaspoons chopped garlic		Salt and pepper to taste
¼	cup fresh parsley	¼	cup Parmesan or Romano cheese

Cook spaghetti according to package directions. Drain, reserving ½ to 1 cup of cooking liquid. Place spaghetti in a large serving dish or bowl.

Sauté garlic and parsley in oil over low heat until garlic is brown. Season with salt and pepper. Pour mixture over cooked spaghetti. Toss, adding reserved cooking liquid as needed if mixture is too dry. Sprinkle with cheese.

4 servings

Sauté seafood, such as salmon or scallops, or vegetables, such as broccoli, with the garlic and parsley for a complete meal.

Spaghetti alla Carbonara

A quick and delicious dinner

1	(16-ounce) package spaghetti	1	(10-ounce) package frozen peas (optional)
2	tablespoons butter	3	eggs
2	tablespoons olive oil	⅓	cup Parmesan cheese
3	slices bacon, diced	⅓	cup Romano cheese
¼	cup fine julienned ham		Black pepper to taste

Cook spaghetti according to package directions. Drain just before mixing with sauce.

Meanwhile, in a saucepan, heat butter and olive oil. Add bacon, ham and peas and sauté until bacon just starts to brown. Beat eggs with cheeses. Remove saucepan from heat and quickly stir in egg mixture. Blend sauce with hot spaghetti. Season with pepper and serve immediately. The eggs will harden slightly from heat of spaghetti.

4 to 6 servings

Stuffed Cannelloni

White Sauce

3	tablespoons butter	½	teaspoon salt
3	tablespoons flour	1¾	cups half-and-half

Filling

1	pound boneless, skinless chicken breast	2	teaspoons tomato paste
2	tablespoons butter	½	teaspoon salt
1	medium onion, chopped	½	teaspoon black pepper
1	clove garlic, minced	½	teaspoon rosemary
2	tablespoons dry white wine	½	teaspoon nutmeg
1	egg	1-1¼	cups chopped fresh spinach

Assembly

1	(28-ounce) jar spaghetti sauce, heated	1	cup grated mozzarella cheese
10	cannelloni shells, approximately, uncooked	½	cup Parmesan cheese

This is my husband's favorite dish - it's time consuming but delicious.

To prepare white sauce, melt butter in a small saucepan. Add flour and salt. Cook and stir until bubbly. Whisk in half-and-half. Cook and stir until sauce thickens and bubbles. Remove from heat and set aside.

For filling, sauté chicken in butter in a medium skillet. Set aside to cool, reserving drippings in skillet. Add onion and garlic to skillet and sauté 5 minutes. Stir in wine and cook 1 to 2 minutes. Transfer to a mixing bowl. Whisk in egg, tomato paste, salt, pepper, rosemary, nutmeg and ⅓ cup of white sauce. Finely chop chicken and add to bowl. Stir in spinach.

To assemble stuffed cannelloni, preheat oven to 350 degrees. Coat the bottom of a 9x13-inch baking pan with ¼ cup spaghetti sauce. Fill each uncooked cannelloni shell with chicken mixture and place in pan. Spoon remainder of white sauce over cannelloni. Top with remaining spaghetti sauce. Sprinkle with cheeses. Bake 35 minutes.

4 to 5 servings

Can be prepared ahead and refrigerated several hours before baking. Can also be frozen.

Vegetables & Grains

Southern Pesto

St. Michael's building just finished was 130 feet long, including the portico, and 60 feet wide; it was of brick with a slate roof.

¼ cup pecans
1-2 cloves garlic
2 cups fresh basil

½ cup Parmesan cheese
½ cup olive oil
Dry pasta

Combine all ingredients except pasta in a food processor. Process until mixture is a smooth paste. Place mixture in the bottom of a pasta serving bowl.

Prepare pasta according to package directions. Drain, reserving ¼ cup of cooking liquid. Add reserved liquid to pesto mixture. Add pasta and toss.

4 to 6 servings

Venten Lasagna

1 large onion, chopped
2 cloves garlic, minced
1 (1-pound) eggplant, diced
4 ounces sliced mushrooms
⅓ cup olive oil
1 (16-ounce) can plum tomatoes, undrained
½ cup dry red wine
¼ cup minced fresh parsley

2 teaspoons oregano
1 teaspoon basil
1 teaspoon salt
½ teaspoon sugar
¼ teaspoon black pepper
9 wide lasagna noodles
1 pound fat-free ricotta cheese
8 ounces fat-free mozzarella cheese, sliced
1½ cups Parmesan cheese

Sauté onion, garlic, eggplant and mushrooms in olive oil over medium heat, stirring frequently, for 15 minutes. Stir in tomatoes, wine, parsley, oregano, basil, salt, sugar and pepper. Bring to a boil. Reduce heat and simmer, covered, for 30 minutes. Uncover and bring to a slow boil. Cook until sauce thickens and reduces to about 5 cups.

Preheat oven to 350 degrees. Cook noodles according to package directions. Spray a 9x13-inch baking dish with nonstick cooking spray.

Spread one-fourth of sauce over bottom of prepared baking dish. Add 3 noodles in a single layer. Spoon a third of ricotta cheese over noodles. Add layers of mozzarella and Parmesan cheeses. Repeat layers twice. Top with remainder of sauce and sprinkle with Parmesan cheese. Bake 30 to 45 minutes or until bubbly.

6 to 8 servings

Vegetables & Grains

Lasagna

2 pounds ground beef
2 pounds sweet Italian
   sausage
2 (28-ounce) jars spicy
   red pepper spaghetti
   sauce
1 (8-ounce) can tomato
   sauce
1 tablespoon sugar
1 egg, beaten
1 (16-ounce) container
   ricotta cheese
   Dried basil to taste

Dried oregano to taste
Garlic powder to taste
2-3 pounds fresh
   mozzarella cheese,
   coarsely grated
½ cup freshly grated
   Romano cheese
½ cup freshly grated
   Parmesan cheese
1 (8-ounce) package
   oven-ready lasagna
   noodles

Brown ground beef and sausage; drain fat. Mix meat with spaghetti sauce, tomato sauce and sugar. Set aside. Mix egg, ricotta cheese, basil, oregano and garlic powder. Set aside.

To assemble, spread a layer of spaghetti sauce over the bottom of a large lasagna pan. Sprinkle with mozzarella, Romano and Parmesan cheeses. Place a layer of uncooked noodles over cheeses. Spread ricotta cheese mixture over noodles. Repeat layers 3 to 4 times, ending with mozzarella cheese. Small chunks of mozzarella on top are nice.

Cover with plastic wrap, then with foil. Refrigerate up to 24 hours or freeze up to 2 months.

When ready to bake, preheat oven to 375 degrees. Remove plastic wrap, replacing foil over top. Bake 40 minutes, or 1½ hours if frozen. Remove foil during final 10 minutes of baking time. Remove from oven and let stand at least 5 minutes before serving.

12 servings

Vegetables & Grains

Shrimp and Sausage Pasta Sauce

1	(16- to 20-ounce) package sweet Italian sausage	1	(8-ounce) can tomato sauce
2	cloves garlic, minced	1	tablespoon basil
1	small onion, chopped	1	pound shrimp, peeled and deveined
2	tablespoons olive oil	1	cup heavy cream
2	(14½-ounce) cans pasta-ready tomatoes		Tabasco sauce to taste
			Salt and pepper to taste

Preheat oven to 350 degrees.

Prick sausages and bake 30 minutes or until thoroughly cooked. Cool slightly and slice.

Sauté garlic and onion in olive oil in a skillet until onion is transparent. Add tomatoes, tomato sauce and basil. Bring to a gentle boil. Add sausage slices and shrimp and cook 5 minutes or until shrimp are pink. Stir in cream and simmer until mixture is heated through.

Season with Tabasco sauce, salt and pepper. Serve over angel hair or your favorite pasta.

6 servings

Tomato, Basil and Mozzarella Pasta

4	tomatoes, chopped	½	cup chopped fresh basil
2	cloves garlic, minced		Olive oil
2	cups grated mozzarella cheese	1	(8-ounce) package spaghetti

Combine tomatoes, garlic, mozzarella and basil in a bowl. Drizzle olive oil over mixture until very moist. Let stand at room temperature for at least 30 minutes.

Cook spaghetti according to package directions; drain. Spoon tomato mixture over hot pasta and serve.

5 to 6 servings

Spinach Pasta

3 cloves garlic, minced
½ onion, chopped
½ tablespoon basil
2 tablespoons pine nuts
   Olive or vegetable oil
     for sautéing
2 (15-ounce) cans stewed
     tomatoes

1 (10-ounce) package
     frozen spinach,
     cooked and
     thoroughly drained
1 (8-ounce) package
     penne pasta
8 ounces feta cheese,
     crumbled

Sauté garlic, onion, basil and pine nuts in oil in a skillet until light brown. Add tomatoes and simmer 10 minutes. Stir in spinach and simmer 10 minutes longer.

Meanwhile, cook pasta according to package directions. Drain and place pasta in a large bowl. Add spinach mixture and toss. Add feta cheese, toss and serve.

4 servings

Spinach Linguine with Cheeses

1½ cups butter
   Pinch of nutmeg
   Pinch of ginger
¼ teaspoon white pepper
4 ounces aged provolone
     cheese, grated
4 ounces fontina cheese,
     cubed
4 ounces Gorgonzola
     cheese, crumbled
1½ cups heavy cream

½ cup mixture of Romano
     and Parmesan cheeses
1 (16-ounce) package
     spinach linguine, or
     1 pound, 10 ounces
     fresh
3 tablespoons finely
     chopped fresh parsley
½ cup mixture of Romano
     and Parmesan cheeses
   Pepper to taste

Melt butter in a heavy 2-quart saucepan. Add nutmeg, ginger, white pepper and provolone, fontina and Gorgonzola cheeses. Cook and stir until cheeses melt. Add the cream and ½ cup Romano and Parmesan cheese mixture. Use a wire whisk to blend ingredients. Bring to a boil and stir until smooth. Remove from heat and keep warm.

Meanwhile, cook linguine until al dente in a large pot. Drain well and return to pot. Pour warm sauce over pasta. Cook and stir over low heat until blended. Top with parsley and ½ cup cheese mixture. Sprinkle with pepper.

6 servings

Pineapple Side Dish

2	(15½-ounce) cans pineapple chunks, undrained	1½	cups grated sharp Cheddar cheese
5	tablespoons flour	1	cup butter cracker crumbs
1	cup sugar	½	cup butter, melted

Preheat oven to 350 degrees.

Pour pineapple with juice into a greased 9x13-inch glass casserole dish.

Combine flour and sugar and sprinkle over pineapple. Mix together cheese and cracker crumbs and spread over pineapple mixture. Drizzle butter over entire casserole. Bake, uncovered, for 45 minutes.

8 to 10 servings

Eliza Lucas Pinckney

One of the first pew holders at St. Michael's was Eliza Lucas Pinckney (1722-1793). She is known for her cultivation of indigo as a major commercial crop for export. In 1744 she married Charles Cotesworth Pinckney (1699-1758), a widower and a statesman. He was one of the first vestrymen at St. Michael's in 1751.

Eliza Lucas Pinckney, like many other plantation ladies, had her own cookbook in 1756. Her cookbook has recipes for various remedies, wine jellies, desserts, meat and poultry, which was typical for a plantation mistress. Here is a recipe from her cookbook.

Little Puddings

Take one quart milk, six eggs, half a nutmeg a teaspoon full of salt and four tablespoons full of flour. Beat the eggs, flour, etc. well together and pour the milk into them just before you put it in the oven. Bake them in half pint bowls, and the same baking that does a custard will be sufficient for them; for sauce, melted butter, a little wine, sugar and nutmeg.

Vegetables & Grains

Meat, Poultry & Game

"...and I am with thee."

Bell Ringers

The bells of St. Michael's arrived
in Charleston from England on the ship,
Little Carpenter, July 15, 1764 and have crossed the
Atlantic several times since. During the Revolution,
the British claimed them as a prize of war. In an ironic
twist, they were burned during the Civil War after
they had been moved to Columbia for safekeeping.
The fragments were sent back to England for recasting.
Most recently they were sent to England yet again
after damage from Hurricane Hugo in 1989. The bells
have pealed hundreds, nay thousands of times sending
the call to worship and declaring the human condition
in times of joy, sadness, peace and unrest. If only
they could talk...ah, but they do!

"And they made bells of pure gold and
put the bells between the pomegranates upon the
hem of the robe, round about between
the pomegranates."
Exodus 39:25

Plantation Supper

1	pound ground beef	1	cup milk	
1	medium onion, chopped		Salt and pepper to taste	
1	(8-ounce) package	1	(16-ounce) can corn,	
	cream cheese, cut into		drained	
	chunks	1	(8-ounce) package egg	
1	(10¾-ounce) can		noodles, cooked	
	condensed cream of			
	mushroom soup			

Brown ground beef and onion in an electric frying pan or a large skillet. Add cream cheese, soup and milk. Cook and stir until cheese melts and mixture is blended. Season with salt and pepper. Stir in corn. Serve over noodles.

4 to 6 servings

In the Lowcountry, ground venison is often used in place of ground beef. Venison was more plentiful than beef in the early days.

Spaghetti Sauce

2	large cloves garlic,	1	teaspoon salt
	minced	1	teaspoon black pepper
1	large onion, chopped	1	tablespoon basil
	Olive oil for sautéing	1	tablespoon oregano
1½	pounds lean ground	1	(28-ounce) can
	chuck		tomatoes, undrained
1	pound mild Italian		and slightly chopped
	sausage		

Sauté garlic and onion in a small amount of olive oil until softened. Add ground chuck and Italian sausage and sauté until browned. Drain.

Stir in salt, pepper, basil, oregano and tomatoes with juice. Simmer 1½ to 2 hours.

4 to 6 servings

Meats, Poultry & Game

137

George's Favorite Meatloaf

Meatloaf

1	pound ground chuck	½	cup finely chopped fresh parsley
1	pound ground pork	½	cup ketchup
½	cup bread crumbs	2	teaspoons mustard
1	large carrot, grated	2	eggs, beaten
1	stalk celery, grated	2	teaspoons salt
½	large onion, finely chopped	1	teaspoon black pepper
2	cloves garlic, crushed	½	teaspoon rosemary

Sauce

3	tablespoons ketchup	2	tablespoons brown sugar
2	teaspoons mustard		

Preheat oven to 400 degrees.

Combine all meatloaf ingredients in a large bowl. Using your hands, knead mixture 1 minute or until thoroughly blended. Form into a loaf in an 11x17-inch pan.

In a small bowl, combine sauce ingredients and mix until smooth. Brush or spoon sauce over meatloaf.

Bake meatloaf 45 to 60 minutes or until a meat thermometer registers 160 degrees. Garnish with fresh rosemary sprigs on top.

Three Cheese Meatloaf

Bread crumbs
3 slices French, Italian or homemade white bread
½ cup milk
2 pounds ground beef
1 large onion, finely chopped
1 clove garlic, finely chopped
2 cups fresh spinach, stemmed, washed, dried and finely chopped
½ cup freshly grated Parmesan cheese
2 tablespoons finely chopped fresh parsley, or 1 teaspoon dried
2 eggs, beaten
2 teaspoons salt
2 teaspoons freshly ground black pepper
1 cup finely diced mozzarella cheese
1 cup slivered Gruyère cheese
Butter

Preheat oven to 350 degrees.

Generously grease a 12x4x2½-inch baking pan. Sprinkle with bread crumbs and shake out excess. Soak bread slices in milk for 5 minutes. Drain milk and squeeze dry bread.

Combine bread slices, beef, onion, garlic, spinach, Parmesan cheese, parsley, eggs, salt and pepper in a large bowl. Mix until well blended.

Divide mixture into 3 portions. Pat one portion into bottom of prepared pan, being sure meat touches sides of pan. Sprinkle mozzarella cheese over top. Make a second meat layer over mozzarella. Cover with Gruyère cheese. Add remaining meat layer, patting to edge of pan. Sprinkle with breadcrumbs and dot with butter.

Bake 1 hour or until cooked through. Remove meatloaf from pan using a large spatula and transfer to a platter. Serve hot or cold.

12 servings

Spinach-Stuffed Meatloaf

Tomato sauce can be drizzled on top of cooked meatloaf.

Meatloaf

1½ pounds extra lean ground beef
1 egg, beaten
½ cup finely crushed herb stuffing mix

2 tablespoons minced onion
½ teaspoon minced garlic

Spinach Filling

1 (10-ounce) package frozen chopped spinach, thawed and drained
4 ounces Cheddar cheese, grated

4 ounces mozzarella cheese, grated
⅓ cup cottage cheese
1 egg, beaten
Parmesan cheese

Preheat oven to 350 degrees.

Combine meatloaf ingredients. Form into a loaf in a 9x13-inch baking pan, making a lengthwise indentation down the middle of the loaf. Bake 30 to 45 minutes or until almost done.

To make spinach filling, mix together spinach, Cheddar, mozzarella and cottage cheeses and egg. Spoon filling into indentation. Bake 5 to 10 minutes longer. Sprinkle with Parmesan cheese and broil 1 to 2 minutes.

4 to 6 servings

Beef Stew
with Herb Dumplings

Beef Stew

⅓	cup flour	2	cups boiling water
1	tablespoon salt	6	potatoes, cut into bite-size pieces
1	teaspoon paprika		
1	teaspoon celery salt	6	carrots, cut into bite-size pieces
¼	teaspoon black pepper		
1½	pounds boneless beef stew meat	2	onions, cut into bite-size pieces
2-4	tablespoons shortening		

Dumplings

1½	cups flour	1	tablespoon shortening
2	teaspoons baking powder	¼	teaspoon celery salt
		¼	teaspoon thyme
¾	teaspoon salt	¾	cup milk

Combine flour, salt, paprika, celery salt and pepper in a plastic bag. Add stew meat and shake to coat meat.

Melt shortening in a Dutch oven. Add meat, reserving flour mixture, and brown on all sides. Add boiling water and simmer over low heat for 2 hours or until meat is tender. Add potatoes, carrots and onions and cook 30 minutes or until vegetables are tender. Stir in reserved flour mixture and cook until broth is thickened. Add dumplings.

To make dumplings, sift together flour, baking powder and salt. Cut in shortening. Add celery salt, thyme and milk. Stir only until ingredients are mixed. Drop by spoonfuls into gently boiling stew. Cook, uncovered, 10 minutes. Cover and cook 10 minutes longer.

Is it not to share your food with the hungry and to provide the poor wanderer with shelter when you see the naked, to clothe him, and not to turn away from your own flesh and blood?

~ Isaiah 58:7

Meats, Poultry & Game

French Beef Stew

When making a stew - beef, lamb or any meat - place a lemon in the pot and let it cook with the stew. The lemon enhances the taste!

2	pounds beef stew meat	½	cup instant tapioca
2	onions, cut into eighths	1	tablespoon sugar
3	stalks celery, cut into 3 to 6 pieces	1	teaspoon basil
4	carrots, cut into thirds		Salt and pepper to taste
2	cups tomato juice	2	large red potatoes, cut into eighths

Preheat oven to 325 degrees.

Combine all ingredients except potatoes in an ovenproof pot or casserole dish. Cover and bake 3 hours. Add potatoes, cover and bake 1 hour longer.

6 servings

Venison or Beef Stew

5	pounds beef or venison stew meat	3	bay leaves
	Vegetable oil	1½	cups red wine
2	large onions, chopped	1	heaping teaspoon oregano
4	cloves garlic, minced or crushed	1	heaping teaspoon basil
4	stalks celery, chopped	2	teaspoons Worcestershire sauce
½	cup flour		Dash of Tabasco sauce
5	beef bouillon cubes		Salt and pepper to taste
10	cups water		

Preheat oven to 350 degrees.

Cook meat, using vegetable oil if needed, in a Dutch oven or turkey roasting pan. When meat starts to brown, add onions and cook until onions become translucent. Stir in garlic and celery and cook 5 to 10 minutes. Sprinkle with flour and mix well. Add bouillon, water, bay leaves, wine, oregano, basil, Worcestershire sauce, Tabasco sauce, salt and pepper.

Bake, uncovered, for 1 to 2 hours or until meat is very tender. Scrape down sides of pan during cooking; these brown bits on the sides of pan add flavor to the stew.

8 servings

Burgundian Beef

2	pounds lean beef, cut into 1-inch cubes	1	teaspoon basil
	Olive oil or bacon fat	1	teaspoon chervil
1	onion, chopped	1	bay leaf
1	carrot, sliced	6	peppercorns
1	teaspoon tarragon		Salt to taste
		2-3	cups Burgundy wine

Brown beef in a small amount of olive oil or bacon fat. Add onion and sauté until softened. Stir in carrot, tarragon, basil, chervil, bay leaf, peppercorns, salt and wine.

Simmer over low heat for at least 1 hour; or 2 hours for even better flavor. Serve over rice.

6 servings

Beef Stroganoff

1	pound beef round steak, thinly sliced	1	(10¾-ounce) can condensed cream of mushroom soup
1	tablespoon oil		
1	onion, sliced	1	soup can water
8	ounces mushrooms, sliced	½	soup can red wine
			Salt and pepper to taste
2	cloves garlic		
1	tablespoon Worcestershire sauce	1	(8-ounce) container sour cream

Brown beef in oil. Add onion and sauté until onion separates into rings. Add mushrooms and garlic and sauté 3 to 5 minutes. Stir in Worcestershire sauce, soup, water, wine, salt and pepper. Simmer 45 to 60 minutes.

Add sour cream just before serving. Serve over rice or egg noodles.

4 servings

Beef Tenderloin

1	beef tenderloin or eye of round, trimmed, any size	2	teaspoons garlic powder
½	cup port or red wine	1½	teaspoon salt
½	cup soy sauce	1	teaspoon black pepper
	Juice of 2 lemons	1	teaspoon dry mustard
4-5	tablespoons parsley	¼	cup sugar

Combine all ingredients in a large plastic zip-top bag. Place bag in a pan or dish in case bag leaks. Marinate beef in refrigerator for 1 to 2 days, turning bag about every 6 to 7 hours.

About 2 hours before cooking, drain beef and bring to room temperature.

When ready to cook, preheat oven to 450 degrees. Roast beef on a rack in a metal pan for 15 minutes. Turn off oven and leave beef in oven for 45 minutes (roast size doesn't matter). Do not open door during this time.

Chuck Meat Marinade

Makes chuck roast taste better than steak!

1	teaspoon ground ginger	¼	cup vegetable oil
1	teaspoon dry mustard	3	cloves garlic
1	teaspoon meat tenderizer	2-3	tablespoons lemon juice
1	tablespoon molasses	1	(3- to 4-pound) beef chuck roast, bone removed
½	cup soy sauce		

Combine all ingredients in a glass dish or zip-top bag. Marinate beef in refrigerator for 48 hours, turning occasionally.

Grill or broil beef, 3 inches from a heat source, for 15 minutes on each side for medium-rare. Cut beef on the vertical into thin slices.

Perfect Roast Beef

1	beef roast, any size	Garlic (optional)
	Salt and pepper	

One hour before cooking, remove roast from refrigerator to bring to room temperature.

Preheat oven to 375 degrees. Rub meat well with salt, pepper and garlic. Place roast in a shallow pan. Do not add water or cover.

Bake 1 hour, then turn off oven. Never open oven door. Turn oven on again to 375 degrees. Bake an additional 30 to 40 minutes just before serving.

The beauty of this recipe is that it can be cooked early in the morning, left in the oven all day, and completed 30 to 40 minutes before serving. It will be crusty and brown on the outside and juicy and pink on the inside.

"Johnny Messetta"

1½ pounds lean ground beef
½ pound pork sausage
1 green bell pepper, chopped
1 large yellow onion, chopped
Salt and pepper to taste
1 (28-ounce) can whole tomatoes, undrained
2 (10¾-ounce) cans condensed tomato soup

Garlic powder to taste
1 tablespoon dry mustard
1 tablespoon light brown sugar
1 (8-ounce) package egg noodles
1 (4½-ounce) jar mushrooms, drained and sliced
1 (7-ounce) jar green olives, drained and sliced
Grated sharp or extra sharp Cheddar cheese

Brown beef, sausage, bell pepper and onion in a skillet; drain. Season with salt and pepper. Add tomatoes with juice, soup, garlic powder, mustard and sugar. Simmer 30 minutes.

Meanwhile, cook noodles according to directions on package; drain well.

When done simmering, preheat oven to 350 degrees. Add mushrooms and olives to beef mixture in skillet. Remove from heat. Combine drained noodles and beef mixture. Pour into a large rectangular baking dish. Sprinkle with cheese. Bake 30 minutes or until bubbly.

Meats, Poultry & Game

145

Hamburger Casserole

1-1½ pounds ground beef
1 medium onion, chopped
8 ounces mushrooms, sliced
1 (6-ounce) package long grain and wild rice mix
1 (8-ounce) can sliced water chestnuts
1 (10½-ounce) can beef consommé
Salt and pepper to taste

Preheat oven to 350 degrees.

Brown beef with onion and mushrooms; drain. Combine beef mixture, rice mix with seasoning packet, water chestnuts, consommé, salt and pepper in a 9x11-inch casserole dish.

Cover and bake 45 minutes. Add extra consommé or water as needed.

6 to 8 servings

Bleu Cheese Burgers Gourmet

¼ cup good bleu cheese
2 tablespoons butter, softened
2 tablespoons finely chopped fresh parsley
1½ pounds ground beef chuck
Salt and pepper to taste
8 (⅓-inch thick) diagonal slices Italian bread
1 clove garlic, halved lengthwise
Olive oil

Puree cheese and butter in a food processor. Add parsley and process until thoroughly blended. Place mixture on wax paper and shape into a log. Freeze at least 20 minutes or until firm.

Divide beef into quarters. Using the ball of your thumb, press one-fourth of butter log into each quarter of meat and form a patty. Season patties with salt and pepper.

Cook patties over high heat on both sides to sear meat. Reduce heat and cook until desired degree of doneness.

Toast bread, rub with garlic, brush with olive oil and toast other side. Serve each patty between 2 slices of toasted bread.

4 servings

Hungarian Stuffed Cabbage

1	(4-pound) head cabbage	1	cup chopped onion
¾	pound ground beef chuck	2	tablespoons vegetable oil
¾	pound ground pork	1	quart water
1	tablespoon salt	2	cups tomato juice
½	teaspoon black pepper	1	(19-ounce) can sauerkraut
1	tablespoon paprika	1	cup sour cream
1¾	cups cooked long-grain rice		

Core cabbage. Place cabbage head in boiling salted water to cover. Remove leaves as they soften and set aside. Trim away thick center vein of each leaf.

Combine beef, pork, salt, pepper, paprika and cooked rice. Sauté onion in vegetable oil and add to meat mixture.

Place a heaping spoonful of meat mixture on each cabbage leaf. Fold in sides, roll up each leaf and place in a large pot. Add 1 quart water and tomato juice. Spread sauerkraut over top of cabbage rolls.

Cover pot and simmer 1½ hours. Just before serving, gently stir in sour cream. Cook until heated but do not boil.

6 to 8 servings

All of the days of the oppressed are wretched, but the cheerful heart has a continual feast.

~ Proverbs 15:15

Beef Burritos

1	cup refried beans	1	cup grated Cheddar cheese
8	(10-inch) flour tortillas, warmed	2	cups shredded lettuce
2	cups cooked shredded beef	2	tomatoes, chopped

Spread 2 tablespoons beans over each tortilla. Cover each with ¼ cup beef. Sprinkle with cheese, lettuce and tomatoes. Fold one end of tortilla over filling and roll up. Eat immediately or heat.

If heating, omit lettuce and tomatoes. Wrap rolled burritos in foil and heat at 350 degrees for 15 minutes.

8 servings

Burrito variations include cooked chicken or ground beef seasoned with taco seasoning, beans and cheese or eggs with sausage or bacon.

Meats, Poultry & Game

147

Margaret Rivers' Hamburger à la Chinois

1	pound ground beef	½	teaspoon garlic salt
2	small onions, sliced	½	teaspoon ground ginger
2	stalks celery, veins removed and diagonally sliced	1½	tablespoons cornstarch
		1	tablespoon soy sauce
1	(8-ounce) package sliced fresh mushrooms, or 1 (8-ounce) can	⅓	cup water, or mushroom juice if canned mushrooms used

Brown beef in its own fat. Add onions, celery and mushrooms and sauté until onions are transparent. Stir in garlic salt, ground ginger, cornstarch, soy sauce and water.

Simmer, adding more water or soy sauce as needed for desired consistency and flavor. Serve over rice. Also good accompanied by glazed fruit or chutney.

4 to 6 servings

Shepherd's Pie

15	pounds ground beef		Salt and pepper to taste
2	medium onions, chopped	10	pounds potatoes
4	(26-ounce) cans condensed cream of mushroom soup	1	cup butter
		1	(16-ounce) container sour cream
2	(32-ounce) bags frozen mixed vegetables	1	pint half-and-half Grated Cheddar cheese

Preheat oven to 350 degrees.

Brown beef with onions in a large skillet in batches, 5 pounds of meat at a time. Drain fat and divide beef into 2 large pans. Divide soup and vegetables equally between the 2 pans. Season with salt and pepper. Mix until combined.

Peel and boil potatoes. Mash potatoes with butter, sour cream and half-and-half until creamy. Season with salt. Spread potatoes over meat mixture. Sprinkle cheese on top. Bake until bubbly.

50 servings

London Broil
with Broiled Tomatoes

1	(2- to 2½-pound, 1½-inch thick) boneless beef top round or shoulder steak	1	teaspoon onion salt
		½	teaspoon garlic powder
		4	small firm tomatoes
		¼	cup bread crumbs
		3	tablespoons Parmesan cheese
¼	cup red wine vinegar	2	tablespoons chopped parsley
¼	cup Worcestershire sauce		
1	teaspoon oregano	¼	teaspoon salt

Place beef in a shallow dish. Combine vinegar, Worcestershire sauce, oregano, onion salt and garlic powder. Mix well and pour over beef. Cover dish with plastic wrap and marinate at room temperature for 2 hours, or refrigerate overnight. Turn meat once while marinating.

Cut tomatoes in half crosswise. Combine bread crumbs, cheese, parsley and salt and stir with a fork to mix. Set aside.

When ready to cook, drain beef, reserving marinade. Place beef on a broiler pan. Broil 4 inches from heat source for about 10 minutes on one side. Turn, brush with marinade, and broil 3 minutes. Place tomatoes, cut-side up, on pan with beef. Baste beef and broil 4 minutes longer. Spoon bread crumb mixture on tomatoes and broil 3 minutes or until bread crumbs are brown and meat is cooked to desired degree of doneness. Let stand several minutes before slicing.

8 servings

Total cooking time for a 1½-inch thick steak is about 10 minutes per side for rare, 12 minutes per side for well done.

Entry from the family Bible of Robert Pringle, Associate Judge of the Court of Common Pleas in the Colony of South Carolina:

"February 1, 1761 ~ This day being Sunday, Divine Service was performed for the first time in the New Church of St. Michael in the Town of Charleston, by the Reverend Mr. Robert Cooper, who was invited to be Minister thereof, and preached a Sermon suitable to the occasion to a crowded congregation, David Deas and myself being the Church Wardens, and on said occasion all my family went to Church and took possession of my Pew there, No. 29, in said Church."

Meats, Poultry & Game

Pork Braised in Whiskey

3	pounds pork loin, boned and tied	⅔	cup bourbon whiskey
18	prunes	½-1	cup beef broth
	Tepid beef broth		Salt and freshly ground black pepper
4	ounces prosciutto or smoked ham, cut into thin slices		Bouquet garni made of thyme, sage and parsley
½	cup Dijon mustard	½	teaspoon arrowroot or cornstarch (optional)
⅔	cup dark brown sugar	1	bunch watercress
2	tablespoons peanut or vegetable oil		

Preheat oven to 375 degrees.

Pat dry meat. Steep prunes in 1 cup tepid broth or enough to cover. Cut prosciutto into strips to fit a larding needle and lard pork loin along its length. If you do not have a larding needle, poke prosciutto into pork with a sharp knife. Brush pork with mustard and roll in brown sugar.

Heat oil in a heavy, ovenproof pot. Add meat and cook 10 to 15 minutes or until browned, being careful not to burn. Add some of the bourbon and set fire to it. When the flame goes out, pour ½ cup broth into the pot. Bake 45 minutes. Turn meat and season with salt and pepper. Add bouquet garni. Reduce heat to 350 degrees. Bake another 45 minutes. Add prunes with steeping liquid and bake 10 to 15 minutes longer.

If pork is to be served hot, remove meat to a warm serving platter. Strain cooking liquid and skim fat. Return liquid to pot and bring to a boil. Add remaining bourbon, stirring to scrape up any sediment. If desired, thicken sauce by adding arrowroot or cornstarch dissolved in cold broth or water. Adjust seasonings as needed.

If pork is to be served cold, add ½ cup broth to cooking liquid and bring to a boil, stirring to scrape up any sediment. Adjust seasonings as needed. Set aside to cool.

To serve in the French manner, slice half of the pork and present it on the serving dish with the unsliced pork. If serving hot, serve the sauce in a sauce boat. If serving cold, the sauce will have jelled. In that case, remove hardened fat, chop jellied sauce and spoon it around the sliced meat. Hot or cold, decorate with prunes and watercress.

Pork and Apple Pie

Serve with spinach salad

1	strip bacon	⅓	cup ale
1	onion, chopped	1	teaspoon sage
2	pounds pork tenderloin, cubed	1	(9-inch) double-crust pie shell, unbaked
2	teaspoons salt	2	cups diced apples
½	teaspoon black pepper	2	tablespoons sugar
2	tablespoons flour	⅛	teaspoon nutmeg

Preheat oven to 425 degrees.

Sauté bacon in a skillet. Remove bacon and reserve for spinach salad. Reserve drippings in skillet. Add onion and sauté. Add pork and cook until browned. Stir in salt and pepper. Sprinkle with flour and stir. Mix in ale and sage. Cool.

Place half of pork mixture in bottom pie crust. Add apples. Sprinkle with sugar and nutmeg. Top with remaining pork mixture. Place top crust over pork. Bake 40 minutes.

4 to 6 servings

Sour Cream Pork Chops

6-8	pork chops	1	(10½-ounce) can consommé
	Sage	1	(8-ounce) container sour cream
	Salt and pepper		
	Vegetable oil	3	tablespoons flour
2	onions, sliced		

Rub pork chops on each side with sage, salt and pepper. Brown pork chops in a skillet in a small amount of vegetable oil. Add onions and consommé. Cover and simmer 30 minutes.

Combine sour cream and flour in a small bowl. Remove pork chops from skillet and add sour cream mixture to skillet. Add pork chops to skillet and simmer, uncovered, until heated through. Serve over rice.

6 to 8 servings

But the fruit of the Spirit is love, joy, peace, patience, kindness, goodness, faithfulness, gentleness, and self-control. Against such things there is no law.

~ Galatians 5:22

Meats, Poultry & Game

This was a favorite growing up. I never found a redeye gravy recipe that I liked so I made this up. You can be flexible on the amount of water, ketchup and coffee and it always comes out great!

Country Ham and Redeye Gravy

1	pound country ham, sliced or chopped	¼-½	cup ketchup
½-¾	cup brewed coffee	1	cup water
¼	teaspoon freshly ground black pepper		Cooked grits

Cook ham in a skillet until slightly browned. Remove ham from skillet. Add coffee to deglaze skillet. Stir in pepper, ketchup and water. Simmer, uncovered, 10 minutes or until gravy reduces by one-third to one-half.

Serve gravy over ham and grits.

2 or 3 servings

Baked Ham Loaf

1	pound smoked ham, ground	½	large onion, finely chopped
8	ounces ground beef round	1½	teaspoons ketchup or chili sauce
1	egg		Salt and pepper to taste
¾	cup cracker crumbs	½	cup tomato juice

Preheat oven to 350 degrees.

Combine all ingredients except tomato juice. Form into a loaf and place in a baking dish. Pour tomato juice over top. Bake 1 to 1½ hours or until done.

3 to 4 servings

This recipe doubles easily. Follow instructions and form into two loaves before baking.

Virginia Ham

1	(14-pound) fresh ham, skin on	1	cup vinegar
1	cup brown sugar		Brown sugar
1	cup molasses		Mustard

Preheat oven to 400 degrees.

Scrub ham with a brush and place in a bowl of cold water, skin-side down. Transfer ham to a roasting pan large enough for liquid to cover ham.

Mix 1 cup brown sugar, molasses and vinegar. Pour over ham with enough water to cover. Cover pan and bake 1 hour or until liquid is boiling. Reduce heat to 325 degrees and bake 1 hour longer. Turn off oven and leave ham in oven, covered, overnight. Do not open oven door!

In the morning, skin ham and add brown sugar and mustard to top. Broil until lightly browned. Cool before slicing.

10 to 12 servings

"BJ's" Bar-B-Q

1	large Boston butt roast		Barbecue sauce
	Salt and pepper to taste		

Place roast in a large Dutch oven. Cover with water and season with salt and pepper. Bring to a boil. Reduce heat, cover and simmer for several hours or until meat is fork-tender.

Remove roast from water and cool. Trim excess fat and shred meat with a fork. Place shredded meat in a baking pan. Cover with barbecue sauce. Bake, covered, at 350 degrees for 1 hour. Uncover pan during last few minutes of cooking.

8 to 10 servings

Heavenly Ham Sauce

Combine ¾ cup apple jelly and 1 tablespoon (or to taste) vinegar in a saucepan. Lightly sprinkle with cinnamon, allspice and ground cloves. Heat until lumps disappear, stirring as needed. Serve with baked ham.

Meats, Poultry & Game

Texas Barbecue

At our farm, the meat was swabbed with this sauce and cooked all night over hickory logs on a huge pit. The sauce was cooked ahead of time in an iron wash pot until it was thick. This oven method gives a pretty good imitation of the pit barbecue.

1 (32-ounce) bottle ketchup
½ cup Worcestershire sauce
1 large onion, chopped
1 large green bell pepper, chopped
½ cup white or cider vinegar
Salt and pepper to taste
4 pounds lean beef, cut into bite-size pieces

Preheat oven to 300 degrees.

Combine ketchup, Worcestershire sauce, onion, bell pepper, vinegar, salt and pepper in a large roasting pan. Mix in beef.

Bake at least 3 hours. Sauce should be thick and meat should be fork-tender.

8 to 12 servings

Use 4 to 8 ounces of raw meat per serving when calculating how much meat you will need.

Meats, Poultry & Game

Grilled Lamb with Thai Sauce

Lamb

1 cup soy sauce
½ cup sugar
3 large cloves garlic, chopped
2 teaspoons chili paste with garlic
1 (2-inch) piece fresh ginger, minced
2 (1¼-pound) racks of lamb, trimmed

Sauce

1 tablespoon peanut oil
¼ cup chopped onion
3 tablespoons chopped celery
2 tablespoons chopped carrot
1 tablespoon curry powder
⅛ teaspoon cayenne pepper
⅛ teaspoon ground coriander
3 cups chicken broth
1 cup beef broth
1 cup heavy cream
½ cup canned coconut milk

Combine soy sauce, sugar, garlic, chili paste and ginger in a medium bowl. Add lamb and turn to coat well. Marinate 1 hour.

To make sauce, heat oil in a large saucepan over medium heat. Add onion, celery and carrot. Sauté 5 minutes or until vegetables are golden and tender. Stir in curry, cayenne pepper and coriander. Whisk in broths. Boil over medium-high heat for 30 minutes or until reduced to 1 cup. Add cream and coconut milk. Reduce heat and simmer 15 minutes or until sauce reduces to 1¼ cups.

To cook, heat grill or broiler to medium-high heat. Drain lamb and cook about 5 minutes on each side for rare. Let stand 10 minutes before cutting lamb into ribs. Meanwhile, reheat sauce. Coat lamb with sauce.

4 servings

Rub for Roasts

4   (3- to 4-inch) sprigs
     fresh rosemary
1   (6- to 8-ounce) jar
     Creole mustard
     Juice of 1 lemon

4   large cloves garlic,
     crushed
     Salt and freshly ground
     black pepper to taste

Blend all ingredients in a food processor. Use as a rub for beef, lamb, pork or venison roasts. Let stand 30 to 60 minutes after applying before cooking.

All-Purpose Marinade

½   cup soy sauce
¼   teaspoon ground
     ginger

¼   cup olive oil
     Garlic cloves to taste
     Black pepper to taste

Combine all ingredients. Store marinade in refrigerator for up to 2 weeks.

Add to chicken, steak, chops or ribs and marinate about 2 hours.

Herb Mint Sauce

½   cup white wine vinegar
½   cup fresh mint
¼   cup fresh basil
¼   cup fresh parsley
6   tablespoons pine nuts

4   cloves garlic, crushed
     and minced, or
     4 teaspoons garlic
     powder
½   cup sugar
¼   cup lemon juice
1   cup olive oil

Combine all ingredients in a blender.

3½ cups

Venison Pie

1-1½ pounds ground venison
Bacon fat
3-4 cloves garlic or to taste, finely chopped
1 large onion, finely chopped
½ teaspoon dried thyme
1 tablespoon dried parsley
¼ teaspoon cayenne pepper
¼-½ teaspoon black pepper or to taste
Salt to taste
1 cup water
¼-⅓ cup dry old-fashioned oats
1 double-crust pie crust

This recipe was given to my brother-in-law from his Canadian friends.

Brown venison in bacon fat. Add garlic, onion, thyme, parsley, cayenne and black peppers, salt and 1 cup water. Cook 30 minutes, adding more water as needed. Cook down to ¼ cup liquid.

Add oats to mixture. Simmer gently, stirring occasionally, for 10 minutes or until liquid is absorbed. Cool to room temperature.

Preheat oven to 350 degrees. Spoon mixture into bottom pie crust. Cover with top crust. Bake 30 to 40 minutes.

4 to 6 servings

Marinated Venison

4-6 pounds venison, preferably loin roast
1 cup soy sauce
1 cup red wine
Juice of 2 lemons
1 tablespoon garlic powder
1 tablespoon onion salt
1 teaspoon tarragon
¼ cup parsley
½ cup sugar

Combine all ingredients in a plastic bag or container. Seal and marinate in refrigerator for 12 to 24 hours.

Grill or bake marinated meat.

Marinated Venison Tenderloin

*Delicious with
a simple
horseradish sauce
of 1 tablespoon
prepared
horseradish and
½ cup mayonnaise.*

4-5 pounds venison tenderloin or roast (or beef)	½ cup gin
	½ cup vegetable oil
1 cup soy sauce	5 cloves garlic, crushed

Combine all ingredients in a plastic zip-top bag. Seal and shake well. Place bag in a bowl and marinate in refrigerator for 24 to 48 hours.

When ready to cook, preheat oven to 350 degrees.

Drain venison and place in a roasting pan. Insert a meat thermometer. Roast 1 hour or until cooked to medium-rare. Cut into thin slices.

6 to 8 servings

Grilled Venison Loin

Venison loin	⅔ cup dry sherry
⅔ cup soy sauce	1 clove garlic
⅔ cup vegetable oil	

Age venison for 1 week.

Combine soy sauce, oil, sherry and garlic to make a marinade. Add loin and marinate 1 hour; marinating longer than 1 hour could cause meat to be too salty.

When ready to cook, preheat grill. Drain meat and grill to desired degree of doneness.

Roasted Loin of Veal with Garlic, Shallots and Mustard Gravy

2-2½	pounds boneless veal loin	12	shallots
	Salt and pepper to taste	½	cup dry white wine
⅓	cup Dijon mustard	2	teaspoons finely chopped fresh tarragon
6	ounces fatback, thinly sliced	¼	cup water
1	head garlic, peeled and separated into cloves	1	teaspoon finely chopped fresh tarragon
			Tarragon sprigs for garnish

Preheat oven to 325 degrees.

Season veal with salt and pepper. Spread mustard over top and sides of veal. Cover top with fatback. Place veal in a roasting pan just large enough to fit. Arrange garlic and shallots in pan. Add wine.

Place on center rack of oven and roast 1 hour, basting every 15 to minutes. Discard fatback and roast 15 to 20 minutes longer or until a meat thermometer registers 150 degrees. Transfer veal to a cutting board and let stand, covered loosely with foil, for 15 minutes.

Use a slotted spoon to transfer garlic and shallots to a small bowl. Toss with 2 teaspoons tarragon. Cover with foil to keep warm.

Skim fat from pan juices. Deglaze pan with ¼ cup water. Cook over high heat, scraping up brown bits, until reduced by half. Strain gravy mixture through a fine sieve into a bowl. Season with salt and pepper.

Cut veal into ½-inch slices and arrange on a serving platter. Scatter garlic and shallot mixture around meat slices. Sprinkle veal with 1 teaspoon tarragon and garnish with tarragon sprigs. Serve gravy on the side.

Grilled Duck Breasts

Delicious!

This dish was prepared and served at the 2000 Honduras Dinner and Auction.

12	boneless, skinless duck breasts	2	(8-ounce) packages cream cheese
1	(16-ounce) bottle Italian dressing	1	(4¼-ounce) jar sliced jalapeño peppers
		1	pound bacon

Soak duck in dressing overnight in refrigerator.

Cut a slice of cream cheese. Press 4 or 5 peppers into cheese. Place cheese between 2 duck breasts. Wrap breasts in 1 or 2 slices of bacon. Repeat with remaining duck breasts.

When ready to cook, preheat grill. Grill breasts until bacon is crisp and duck is browned. Serve with rice cooked in beef broth.

4 to 6 servings

Caroline Russell's Roasted Duck

¼	cup diced celery	1½	cups water
¼	cup diced green bell pepper	1	teaspoon salt
	Oil for sautéing	1	cup dry converted rice
1	pound country sausage, casings removed	2	ducks, washed
			Salt and pepper to taste
		¼	cup water
		4	slices bacon

Sauté celery and bell pepper in oil. In a separate pan, brown, drain and crumble sausage. Combine sautéed vegetables, sausage, 1½ cups water, salt and rice in a rice steamer. Steam until rice is three-fourths cooked.

Preheat oven to 325 degrees.

Season ducks with salt and pepper. Stuff cavities with rice mixture and secure with toothpicks. Place stuffed ducks in a roasting pan. Add ¼ cup water to pan and place 2 slices bacon on each duck. Bake 2 to 2½ hours or until fork-tender.

Tropical Duck

2	ducks		Juice of 2 oranges
	Salt and pepper to taste	2	heaping teaspoons
1	orange, cut into		guava jelly or
	6 wedges		marmalade
1	large onion, cut into	½	bottle red wine
	6 wedges		

Preheat oven to 250 degrees.

Season inside and out of ducks with salt and pepper. Divide orange and onion wedges between duck cavities. Place ducks, breast-side up, in a roasting pan.

Squeeze orange juice over each duck, using 1 orange per duck. Top each duck with a heaping teaspoon of jelly. Add wine to pan. Seal pan tightly with foil. Bake 5 hours.

6 to 8 servings

Walnut Quail

12	quail	1	cup chopped walnuts
¾	cup butter	1	cup sliced mushrooms
	Salt and pepper to taste	1	cup heavy cream
1	cup chopped onion or	1	cup white wine
	shallot		

Sauté quail in butter. Season with salt and pepper. Add onion, walnuts and mushrooms and sauté briefly.

Add cream and wine. Cook over medium-low heat for 45 minutes.

6 servings

Turkey Steamed in Wine

This is the way I have prepared my turkey for the last 25 years, and would never consider any other way. The preparation time is about 40 minutes - then just sit back and relax. When complete, you will enjoy the most moist and flavorful turkey you have ever prepared.

1	(12- to 15-pound) turkey, completely thawed	½	cup chopped fresh parsley
1	small onion, quartered	2	(10¾-ounce) cans onion soup
1	teaspoon salt	1	soup can white wine
1	carrot, cut into pieces	½	teaspoon salt
1	apple, cut into pieces	1	teaspoon thyme
1-2	stalks celery, cut into pieces		Melted butter

Preheat oven to 400 degrees.

Tear two 24-inch sheets of heavy-duty foil. Fold and seal sheets together along long edges. Grease foil with oil. Place turkey on foil in a roasting pan.

Place onion and 1 teaspoon salt in turkey's neck cavity. Fold skin flap over cavity. Combine carrot, apple, celery, parsley, soup, wine, salt and thyme in body cavity. Baste turkey with melted butter.

Tent a third sheet of foil over top of turkey, keeping foil from touching turkey. Pinch edges of foil sheets together, sealing well to prevent steam from escaping.

Place turkey on lowest shelf of oven. Bake 5 minutes per pound plus 15 minutes. Remove top piece of foil and bake, uncovered, 5 minutes per pound plus 15 minutes.

Barbeque Turkey

Great for parties!

2	cups vinegar	1	tablespoon salt
4	tablespoons butter	1	tablespoon black pepper
3	tablespoons ketchup	2	large onions, chopped
3	tablespoons Worcestershire sauce	2	dashes garlic powder
3	tablespoons Tabasco sauce	1	turkey breast, skinless, bone-in

Combine all ingredients except turkey in a large pot. Cook sauce mixture 15 minutes. Place turkey in sauce, cavity-side down. Cook on stovetop for 2 to 3 hours.

Remove bone and shred meat with 2 forks. Return meat to sauce and cook 1½ hours longer.

Turkey Breast with Best Fresh Sauce

1	(8-pound) turkey breast, thawed	4	teaspoons minced garlic
½	cup dry white wine	1	tablespoon fresh thyme, or 1 teaspoon dried
¼	cup dark sesame oil	1	teaspoon cayenne pepper
¼	cup soy sauce	1	tablespoon minced fresh ginger
3	tablespoons fresh lime juice		

Sauce

2½	cups mayonnaise	1½	tablespoons finely chopped and seeded fresh jalapeño
½	cup finely chopped fresh cilantro	1	tablespoon soy sauce
3	tablespoons fresh lime juice	2	teaspoons minced garlic
		1½	teaspoons Dijon mustard

Remove skin and bone from turkey breast. Cut breast in half. Combine wine, sesame oil, soy sauce, lime juice, garlic, thyme, cayenne pepper and ginger in a shallow dish. Add turkey breast halves and turn to coat. Marinate 2 hours at room temperature, or at least 12 hours in the refrigerator.

Meanwhile, or while turkey bakes, mix together all sauce ingredients. Set aside or refrigerate.

When ready to cook, remove turkey from marinade, reserving marinade. Place turkey, skinned-side up, in a shallow roasting pan.

Broil 2 to 3 inches from heat source for 10 minutes or until browned. Pour reserved marinade over turkey and bake at 375 degrees for 1 hour or until a meat thermometer registers 180 degrees in the thickest part of the meat. Remove from oven and let stand 10 minutes before slicing. Garnish with lime wedges and fresh cilantro leaves. Serve sauce on side.

12 servings

Serve anytime for a meal and great leftover for sandwiches or salad.

Gladys' Giblet Gravy

Bacon Drippings (from 4 slices bacon)

3 tablespoons flour

2 cups turkey essence

2 cups water

Meat from gizzard and neck

In a large skillet fry 4 slices of bacon. Remove bacon and to drippings add flour. Stir in turkey essence and water. Add meat from neck bone and gizzard, simmer to desired consistency adding essence and water as needed.

Note: You can also add the liver to the gravy but it adds a strong flavor. I like to add meat from the thigh.

Meats, Poultry & Game

163

Chicken with Capers

Delicious served cold.

I use skinless, bone-in chicken for this recipe, but it may be done in a variety of ways. For tailgate parties, use skinless drumsticks.

2	tablespoons olive oil	2	tablespoons fresh basil
2	tablespoons butter	2	tablespoons fresh thyme
1	chicken, cut into pieces	2	(14½-ounce) cans diced tomatoes, undrained
2-3	cloves garlic or to taste, crushed	½	cup capers
1	large onion, thinly sliced		Salt and pepper to taste
1	cup dry white wine		
1-1½	(14½-ounce) cans chicken broth		

Preheat oven to 350 degrees.

Heat oil and butter in a skillet. Add chicken and sauté until lightly browned. Transfer chicken to a casserole dish.

Add garlic and onion to skillet and reduce heat. Sauté, being careful not to burn garlic. Add wine, broth, basil and thyme. Increase heat and cook until liquid reduces. Lower heat and add tomatoes with juice. Pour mixture over chicken in dish.

Bake 1 hour. Add capers just before serving. Season with salt and pepper. Serve chicken and sauce over rice.

For extra spice, canned tomatoes and green chilies can be used to replace half of the tomatoes.

Meats, Poultry & Game

164

Country Captain Chicken

1	chicken, any size, or a turkey breast	1	teaspoon salt
2	cups cooked rice	1	cup raisins
1	large onion, chopped	1	cup slivered almonds
1	green bell pepper, chopped	1	(16-ounce) can tomato puree
1-2	teaspoons curry powder	1	(8-ounce) can tomato sauce

Boil chicken. When cooled, discard skin and bones and cut meat into bite-size pieces. Combine chicken with rice, onion, bell pepper, curry powder, salt, raisins, almonds, tomato puree and tomato sauce in a large Dutch oven.

Cook over medium heat on the stove or at 350 degrees in the oven for about 1 hour.

6 hungry or 8 regularly polite people

For extra flavor, use broth from boiling chicken to cook the rice.

This recipe reheats beautifully and is great for a crowd.

Chicken with Sun-Dried Tomatoes

4	boneless, skinless chicken breasts, cut into strips	⅔	cup heavy cream
1½	tablespoons butter	2	tablespoons vermouth or white wine
1	large shallot, minced, or 2 tablespoons minced onion	1-2	tablespoons dried tarragon
1	tablespoon Dijon mustard	3	ounces sun-dried tomatoes

Sauté chicken strips in butter in a skillet. Remove chicken and set aside. Add shallot to skillet and sauté 1 minute. Add mustard, cream, vermouth, tarragon and tomatoes to skillet.

Cook and stir until sauce thickens slightly. Return chicken to skillet and simmer until heated through. Serve with rice or pasta.

St. Michael's Staff Party Chicken

This recipe was given to me by Mary Larsen, wife of Father Kal—both "Sainted" members of St. Michael's Church.

Mary and Kal hosted the St. Michael's staff Christmas party for years and served this delicious chicken dish. When the Christmas party moved to the Rectory, I continued their tradition of serving this wonderful recipe.

Thanks be to God for those special gatherings that are blessed because they reflect God's love in our lives.

13	boneless chicken breast halves	2	(10¾-ounce) cans condensed cream of mushroom soup
13	slices bacon	2	(8-ounce) containers sour cream
1	(10-ounce) can chipped beef		Paprika

Preheat oven to 275 degrees.

Wrap each chicken breast with a slice of bacon and secure with a toothpick. Spread chipped beef over the bottom of two 8x12-inch glass baking dishes. Arrange chicken on top.

Mix soup and sour cream and pour over chicken. Sprinkle with paprika. Bake, uncovered, for 3 hours.

Opulent Chicken
Excellent over pasta or rice

4	chicken breasts	2	tablespoons flour
1½	teaspoons salt	1	(10½-ounce) can chicken consommé
¼	teaspoon black pepper		
1	teaspoon paprika	¼-½	cup cooking sherry
½	cup margarine, divided	1	(14-ounce) can artichoke hearts
4	cups sliced mushrooms, or 2 (6-ounce) cans		

Preheat oven to 375 degrees.

Sprinkle chicken with a mixture of salt, pepper and paprika, making more of seasoning mixture as needed. Brown chicken in 4 tablespoons margarine in a skillet. Transfer chicken to a casserole dish.

Add remaining 4 tablespoons margarine to skillet. Add mushrooms and sauté about 5 minutes. Sprinkle flour over mushrooms and stir in consommé and sherry. Simmer sauce 5 minutes. Repeat sauce steps if more is desired.

Arrange artichoke hearts among chicken in dish. Pour mushroom sauce over chicken. Bake, covered, for 45 minutes.

Meats, Poultry & Game

Chicken in Wine

A gourmet's treasure!

3	whole chicken breasts, boned	1	(8-ounce) can sliced water chestnuts, drained
	Salt and pepper to taste	2	tablespoons chopped green bell pepper
4	tablespoons butter		
1	(10¾-ounce) can cream of chicken soup	1	(3-ounce) can mushrooms, drained
¾	cup Sauterne wine	¼	teaspoon thyme

Preheat oven to 350 degrees.

Lightly season chicken with salt and pepper. Brown chicken in butter in a skillet. Transfer chicken to a shallow baking dish.

Add soup to skillet drippings. Slowly mix in wine and stir until smooth. Bring to a boil and pour over chicken. Sprinkle water chestnuts and bell pepper over chicken. Add mushrooms and thyme and cover. Bake 25 minutes. Uncover and bake 20 to 30 minutes longer. Serve with wild or white rice.

4 servings

Stuffed Chicken

½	cup ricotta cheese	1	(10-ounce) package frozen chopped spinach, thawed and drained
¼	cup grated mozzarella cheese		
4	boneless, skinless chicken cutlets	2	eggs, beaten
4	ounces prosciutto ham, thinly sliced	1	cup seasoned bread crumbs

Preheat oven to 375 degrees.

Combine cheeses. Layer each cutlet with ham, spinach and cheese mixture. Roll up chicken and secure with toothpicks.

Dip each chicken roll in egg, then coat with bread crumbs. Bake 35 minutes.

4 servings

Sautéed Chicken Cutlets with Vegetable Rice

A good "for two" dinner

When my father was stationed in Germany in the Army, my mother had a cook each evening who would announce "The potatoes are peeled, what should I prepare for dinner?" She could not be persuaded to have a potato free meal - Mother gave up trying. This dish is a good substitute. Many people in Charleston have a similar view concerning rice!

Chicken

2	boneless, skinless chicken breast halves	¼	cup Parmesan cheese
	Salt and pepper to taste	1	egg, beaten
½	cup bread crumbs	3	tablespoons butter, melted

Rice and Vegetables

	Long-grain white rice	2-3	cloves garlic, minced
	Chicken broth	¼-⅓	cup sliced red bell pepper
	Butter		
4	small fresh mushrooms, sliced	¼-⅓	cup sliced green bell pepper
	Salt and pepper to taste	¼-⅓	cup finely chopped celery
2-3	tablespoons olive oil		
¼-⅓	cup finely chopped onion		Italian seasoning to taste

Use a meat mallet or rolling pin to flatten chicken between wax paper to ¼-inch thickness. Season with salt and pepper. Combine bread crumbs and cheese. Dip chicken in egg, then coat with crumb mixture. Sauté chicken in butter 4 minutes on each side or until well-browned and tender. Remove from pan and keep warm, reserving pan drippings.

To make rice, prepare according to package directions using chicken broth instead of water; keep warm.

Add butter to drippings in chicken pan. Add mushrooms and sauté. Season with salt and pepper. Remove mushrooms. Add olive oil and onion to pan. Sauté until softened. Add garlic and sauté briefly. Return mushrooms to pan. Add bell peppers and celery and sauté until vegetables are crisp-tender. Add extra butter or olive oil as needed to prevent sticking. Season with salt, pepper and Italian seasoning.

To serve, mound rice on individual serving plates. Top with vegetable mixture. Place chicken breast on the side.

2 servings

Meats, Poultry & Game

Chicken with Walnuts

Different and Delicious

1 pound boneless, skinless chicken breast, cubed into bite-size pieces	Vegetable oil
	2 cups halved walnuts
Salt to taste	1 teaspoon sugar
1 tablespoon flour	1 tablespoon soy sauce
1 egg white, lightly beaten	2 tablespoons dry sherry or rice wine

Rub chicken with a mixture of salt and flour. Pour egg white over chicken to coat. Stir-fry chicken in oil in a skillet for 2 minutes. Remove chicken from skillet, reserving drippings in skillet.

Add walnuts to skillet and stir-fry 1 minute. Return chicken to skillet and cook 1 minute longer. Add sugar, soy sauce and sherry to skillet and cook 1 to 2 minutes.

4 to 6 servings

The first thing I remember about dinnertime was the necessity to always thank God for it all.

Poppy Seed Chicken

4 boneless, skinless chicken breasts, cut into pieces	1 sleeve Ritz crackers, crushed
1 cup sour cream	½ cup butter
1 (10¾-ounce) can condensed cream of chicken soup	3 tablespoons poppy seeds

Season chicken and cook until done. Combine cooked chicken with sour cream and soup. Place in a 9-inch square baking dish.

Preheat oven to 350 degrees.

Brown cracker crumbs in butter and sprinkle over chicken mixture. Top with poppy seeds. Bake 30 minutes.

4 servings

Meats, Poultry & Game

Chicken Rosemary

This is the dish I always take to friends, neighbors or relatives who are sick and need a soothing meal.

4	skinless chicken breasts	½	teaspoon salt
2	cloves garlic, crushed		Black pepper to taste
3	tablespoons vegetable oil	½	cup dry white wine
3	tablespoons butter or margarine	½	cup chicken broth
½	teaspoon rosemary	¼	cup heavy cream
			Chopped fresh parsley for garnish (optional)

Over medium-high heat, sauté chicken and garlic in oil and butter until well-browned in a heavy skillet with a domed lid. Discard garlic. Add rosemary, salt, pepper, wine and broth. Bring to a boil. Reduce heat and cover. Simmer 25 to 35 minutes or until fork-tender, turning chicken once.

Transfer chicken to a warm serving platter. Boil liquid in skillet over high heat until reduced by half. Reduce heat and stir in cream until blended. Cook sauce until heated through and slightly thickened. Pour sauce over chicken. Sprinkle with parsley and serve immediately.

4 servings

Curried Chicken

As given by U.S. Navy Master Chief Stewards Mate H. T. Hightower, who cooked for President Harry S. Truman aboard the Presidential yacht, "Williamsburg".

1	(10¾-ounce) can condensed cream of chicken soup	2	teaspoons curry powder or to taste
		¾	cup light cream
1	(10¾-ounce) can condensed cream of mushroom soup	2	cups diced cooked chicken
		½	cup broken cashew nuts

Toppings

Finely chopped cooked bacon
Minced onion
Chopped hard-cooked egg yolk
Chopped hard-cooked egg white

Coconut
Chopped green bell pepper
Chopped ripe tomato
Chopped celery
Chutney

Combine soups, curry powder and cream in the top of a double boiler. Cover and heat, stirring occasionally.

Add chicken and heat. Sprinkle with nuts. Serve over hot cooked rice with toppings in separate bowls on the side.

4 servings

Meats, Poultry & Game

Chicken Sauté Linguine

1	clove garlic, chopped	1	(14½-ounce) can chicken broth
¼	teaspoon grated fresh ginger	2	tablespoons soy sauce
1	Vidalia onion, chopped Olive oil	2	tablespoons white wine Dash of cayenne pepper
1-3	boneless, skinless whole chicken breasts, cut into bite-size pieces	¼	cup smooth peanut butter Linguine
1-2	tablespoons cornstarch	3	green onions, green part only, chopped

Preheat oven to 350 degrees.

Sauté garlic, ginger and onion in olive oil until onion softens. Remove mixture and set aside, reserving drippings in skillet. Toss chicken with cornstarch. Add chicken to skillet and cook until brown. Return onion mixture to skillet.

In a mixing bowl, combine broth, soy sauce, wine and cayenne pepper. Blend in peanut butter. Pour into skillet. Cook 10 minutes over medium heat. Place skillet in oven and bake 10 minutes longer.

Meanwhile, cook linguine according to package directions; drain. Toss linguine with chicken mixture. Sprinkle with green onions.

4 to 6 servings

Spicy "Oven Fried" Chicken

Good served warm or cold

1¼ cups buttermilk
¼ cup extra virgin olive oil
3 tablespoons hot pepper sauce
2 tablespoons Dijon mustard
2 cloves garlic, minced
1 teaspoon salt or to taste
1½ teaspoons black pepper
1 large onion, sliced
12 pieces boneless, skinless chicken

1 cup plain dry bread crumbs
⅓ cup freshly grated Parmesan cheese
¼ cup flour
2 teaspoons dried thyme
½ teaspoon paprika
½ teaspoon cayenne pepper
½ teaspoon salt
3 tablespoons butter, melted

Whisk together buttermilk, olive oil, pepper sauce, mustard, garlic, 1 teaspoon salt and black pepper in a dish or plastic zip-top bag. Add onion and chicken and marinate in refrigerator at least 3 or up to 24 hours, turning chicken occasionally.

Combine bread crumbs, cheese, flour, thyme, paprika, cayenne pepper and ½ teaspoon salt.

When ready to cook, drain chicken. Coat chicken in bread crumb mixture and let stand 30 minutes in a baking dish.

Preheat oven to 425 degrees. Drizzle butter over chicken. Bake 50 minutes or until crisp and golden.

David's Chicken

1 chicken breast per person
Spinach leaves, blanched

Boursin cheese, rolled into a "cheese log"
Salt and pepper to taste
½ cup crushed nuts per person

Preheat oven to 350 degrees.

Pound chicken thin. Salt and pepper. Place several blanched leaves on chicken breast. Roll "cheese log" in crushed nuts and place on spinach at one end. Roll tight.

Place seam side down in casserole dish. Bake 35 to 45 minutes.

Drain juices. Before serving, cover chicken with Raspberry Vinaigrette.

Seafood

"Fishes and Loaves"

Cross at Kanuga

There are places on God's green earth
that speak to generation after generation. Thus it
is at the cross at Camp Kanuga in Hendersonville,
North Carolina where St. Michaelites have retreated
for reflection and fellowship, not to mention a respite
from the Lowcountry summer. Spiritual awakening,
yes! When one looks out over those Smoky Mountain
foothills, God's awesome nature seems so close you can
taste it. We are but tiny specks and we are saved.

"I will lift mine eyes unto the hills, from whence
cometh my help. My help cometh from the
Lord, which made heaven and earth."
Psalm 121:1-2

Grilled Salmon

Lay open a boned whole salmon on double-wide, heavy-duty foil on a preheated grill. Cover salmon with slices of orange, lemon and lime along with any collected juices from the fruit. Add slices of onion and a splash or two of Rhine wine. Fold foil over salmon.

Grill 25 minutes or until salmon flakes easily with a fork. Cooking time will depend on heat of coals.

6 to 8 servings

And He directed the people to sit down on the grass. Taking the five loaves and the two fish and looking up to Heaven, He gave thanks and broke the loaves.

~ Matthew 14:19

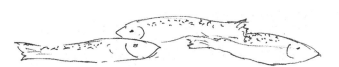

Baked Fillet of Sole

½ cup butter	½ tablespoon Dijon mustard
1 tablespoon vinegar	
1 tablespoon fresh lemon juice	1½ pounds fillet of sole
	Bread crumbs
1 tablespoon Worcestershire sauce	Chopped parsley

Preheat oven to 400 degrees.

Melt butter in a small saucepan. Add vinegar, lemon juice, Worcestershire sauce and mustard. Stir until combined.

Roll sole fillets in bread crumbs and place in a shallow baking dish without overlapping. Pour sauce mixture over fillets. Bake 20 minutes. Garnish with chopped parsley and serve immediately.

4 servings

Seafood

173

Oven-Fried Catfish

This recipe works beautifully with any white fish like orange roughy, tilapia or flounder. Be sure to adjust the time and temperature for thinner fish.

Plain dry bread crumbs
4 large fresh catfish fillets
6 tablespoons reduced-fat sour cream
2 teaspoons canola oil
1 tablespoon fresh lemon juice
¾ teaspoon paprika
½ teaspoon salt
¾ teaspoon black pepper

Preheat oven to 475 degrees.

Wash and pat dry fish with paper towels. Sprinkle some bread crumbs on a 24-inch sheet of wax paper. Place catfish fillets on another 24-inch sheet of wax paper.

Combine sour cream, oil, lemon juice, paprika, salt and pepper. Spread over each fillet. Sprinkle with bread crumbs and pat down so crumbs stick. Turn fillets onto wax paper with bread crumbs. Spread sour cream mixture on other side of fillets. Sprinkle with more bread crumbs and pat down.

Place fish on a baking sheet lightly greased with canola oil, leaving at least an inch between fillets. Bake 20 minutes or until fish is nicely browned and flakes easily with a fork.

4 to 5 servings

Devine Fish Fillets

Very quick and easy!

½ cup butter
6 white fish fillets
1 egg, beaten
Cracker crumbs
Juice of 1 lemon

Preheat oven to 450 to 500 degrees. While heating, melt butter in oven in a glass baking dish. Leave in oven until butter browns, being careful not to burn.

Dip fillets in egg, then roll in cracker crumbs. Place fillets in baking dish, coating both sides with browned butter. Squeeze lemon juice on top. Bake a few minutes or until just barely done.

6 servings

Peg's No-Fail Crawfish Étouffée

½ cup butter
6 tablespoons flour
1 cup chopped onion
1-2 bunches green onions, chopped
½ cup chopped bell pepper
1 cup ribbed and minced celery
¼ cup olive oil
1-2 bay leaves
¼-½ cup chopped parsley

Tabasco sauce to taste
1 cup chicken broth or water
3 pounds peeled crawfish plus the fat, or substitute 1 teaspoon tomato paste for color if crawfish fat not available
Cornstarch

Melt butter in a skillet and stir in flour. Cook and stir until mixture turns into a rich brown colored roux. Cool.

Sauté onions, bell pepper and celery in olive oil until softened and transparent. Stir sautéed vegetables into roux. Add bay leaves, parsley, Tabasco sauce, broth and crawfish with fat. Simmer until crawfish are cooked. Use a mixture of cornstarch and water to thicken as desired. Serve over rice.

6 servings

Shrimp or a combination of crawfish and shrimp can be used.

Sour Cream Shrimp

½ cup butter
6 large bunches green onions, green part only, chopped
1 bunch parsley, stemmed and chopped
1 tablespoon fresh or dried dill

1-2 cloves garlic, pressed, or 2 teaspoons minced
1 teaspoon dry mustard
1½ pounds shrimp
12 ounces sour cream, room temperature

Melt butter in a large skillet. Stir in green onions, parsley, dill, garlic and mustard. Add shrimp and cook until shrimp are pink. Cool.

Add sour cream. Cover and bring to a slight boil. Serve immediately over rice.

6 servings

Martha's Shrimp and Rice Casserole

You can substitute chicken for shrimp in this recipe or use feta cheese instead of Cheddar.

1	pound mushrooms, sliced	2	pounds cooked and peeled shrimp
½	cup sliced green bell pepper	1	cup grated sharp Cheddar cheese
½	cup sliced onion	1	(10¾-ounce) can condensed cream of mushroom soup
½	cup diced celery		
	Butter for sautéing		
1	cup dry rice, cooked	3	lemons, thinly sliced

Preheat oven to 375 degrees.

Sauté mushrooms, bell pepper, onion and celery in butter until tender. Combine sautéed vegetables with cooked rice, shrimp, cheese and soup.

Place in a greased casserole dish. Cover with lemon slices. Bake 30 minutes.

4 to 6 servings

Tigger's Shrimp Casserole

1-2	pounds raw shrimp, peeled and deveined	1	teaspoon prepared mustard
½-1	cup dry sherry	1	pound processed cheese loaf, cubed
5	tablespoons butter		
3	tablespoons flour	2	tomatoes, sliced
2	cups milk	½	cup bread crumbs
	Salt and pepper to taste	8	slices bacon, cooked and crumbled
1	teaspoon Worcestershire sauce		

Soak shrimp in sherry 30 to 45 minutes.

Preheat oven to 350 degrees. Melt butter in a saucepan. Stir in flour until smooth. Whisk in milk. Cook and stir until sauce thickens. Season with salt and pepper. Add Worcestershire sauce and mustard. Stir in cheese until melted. Add shrimp with at least ½ cup of sherry soaking liquid and stir.

Pour mixture into a 3-quart casserole dish. Top with tomato slices and bread crumbs. Sprinkle with bacon. Bake 30 to 45 minutes.

4 to 6 servings

Seafood

Shrimp and Sausage in Brown Gravy

8	ounces bacon		½	(16-ounce) package Polish sausage, sliced into bite-size rounds
1	small onion, chopped			Seasoned salt to taste
½	green bell pepper, chopped		3-5	drops browning and seasoning sauce
¼	cup flour			
3	cups water			
1½	pounds raw shrimp			

Cook bacon in a large skillet. Remove bacon and set aside for another use, reserving drippings in skillet. Add onion and bell pepper to drippings and sauté. Stir in flour over low heat to make a roux. In a slow stream, stir in water to make a sauce.

Add shrimp and sausage. Cook over low to medium heat until shrimp are pink. Add seasoned salt and browning sauce. Simmer 20 minutes. Serve with grits.

6 servings

At holidays we always have "poppers"...we put on the paper party hats from inside the poppers and go around the table reading our jokes and trying to exchange our plastic prizes (if someone has one that we might like better than the one we received!)

Rice and Shrimp Pilau
"Simple"

8	slices bacon	2	cups raw shrimp, peeled
½	cup chopped onion		Flour
½	cup chopped celery		Salt and pepper to taste
½	cup chopped green bell pepper	3	cups steamed rice

Cook bacon in a skillet. Remove bacon, crumble and set aside, reserving bacon drippings in a bowl.

Sauté onion, celery and bell pepper in skillet in 1 tablespoon of bacon drippings. Remove vegetables. Add 2 tablespoons bacon drippings to skillet. Add shrimp and sauté until pink. Sprinkle shrimp with a light coating of a mixture of flour, salt and pepper.

Add sautéed vegetables to shrimp in skillet and cook briefly. Serve over steamed rice with crumbled bacon sprinkled on top.

4 servings

Seafood

Thai Shrimp and Sesame Noodles

1	pound raw shrimp, peeled and deveined
1	(8-ounce) bottle light Italian salad dressing, divided
2	tablespoons chunky peanut butter
1	tablespoon soy sauce
1	tablespoon honey
1	teaspoon grated ginger
½	teaspoon crushed red pepper flakes
1	(8-ounce) package pasta of your choice
2	tablespoons olive oil
1	tablespoon sesame oil
1	medium carrot, grated
1	cup chopped green onion
2	tablespoons chopped parsley

Combine shrimp and ⅓ cup salad dressing in a medium bowl. Cover and refrigerate 1 hour.

In a small bowl, whisk together peanut butter, soy sauce, honey, ginger, pepper flakes and remainder of salad dressing. Prepare pasta according to package directions; drain.

In a 4-quart saucepan, heat olive and sesame oils until hot. Add carrot and cook 1 minute. Add shrimp and green onion and cook 3 minutes or until shrimp are pink.

In a large bowl, toss pasta with peanut butter mixture, shrimp mixture and chopped parsley.

4 to 6 servings

Shrimp Orleans

½	cup butter
1	pound raw shrimp, peeled and deveined
1	(8-ounce) container sour cream
1	tablespoon ketchup
1	tablespoon Worcestershire sauce
	Garlic salt to taste
	Black pepper to taste
1	tablespoon cooking sherry

Melt butter in a 2-quart saucepan or skillet. Add shrimp and sauté until pink.

Stir in sour cream, ketchup, Worcestershire sauce, garlic salt, pepper and sherry. Serve over rice.

4 servings

Jambalaya

4 tablespoons butter
2 large onions, minced
2 green bell peppers, chopped
1 bunch celery, chopped
2 cups sliced okra
4 cups peeled and chopped tomatoes
8 ounces ham, cut into bite-size pieces
1 bunch parsley, chopped
2 tablespoons tomato paste

1 cup chicken broth
1½ pounds raw shrimp, peeled and deveined
1 pint oysters (optional)
1½ cups dry rice
2½ cups chopped cooked chicken
6 dashes Tabasco sauce
½ teaspoon mace
Salt to taste
½ cup buttered bread crumbs

Melt butter in a large saucepan. Add onions, bell peppers, celery and okra and sauté. Add tomatoes, ham, parsley, tomato paste and broth. Simmer 1½ hours.

Stir in shrimp and oysters. Simmer 10 minutes. In a separate saucepan, cook rice 5 minutes. Add partially cooked rice and chicken to jambalaya. Cook 10 minutes or until sauce is thickened.

Preheat oven to 350 degrees. Stir Tabasco sauce, mace and salt into mixture. Pour into a casserole dish. Top with buttered bread crumbs. Bake 30 minutes.

10 to 12 servings

This recipe is one that I have had for a number of years and both friends and family enjoy it. It is basically a Louisiana dish but many variations of this are used in other parts of the South and in South Carolina. I have seen it cooked with just chicken or shrimp. I have also eaten this dish with sausage in it. All variations are very good, but the above is my favorite.

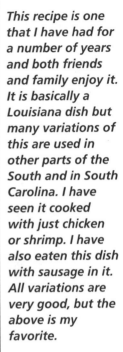

Seafood

179

Jambalaya

2	tablespoons butter	1	teaspoon chili powder
1	cup chopped onion	1	teaspoon salt
2	green bell peppers, chopped	½	teaspoon black pepper
		½	cup white wine
2	cloves garlic, minced	1½	cups chicken broth
1	cup dry rice	2	cups diced ham
1	(19-ounce) can tomatoes, drained and chopped	½-1	pound smoked sausage, sliced and browned
½	teaspoon thyme	1	pound shrimp
¼	teaspoon basil		Butter
¼	teaspoon paprika		

Preheat oven to 350 degrees.

Melt butter in a large ovenproof skillet. Add onion and bell pepper and sauté. Add garlic and sauté. Add rice and cook and stir until opaque. Add tomatoes, thyme, basil, paprika, chili powder, salt, black pepper, wine, broth, ham and browned sausage. Cover and bake 35 minutes or until rice is plump and liquid is absorbed.

Meanwhile, sauté shrimp in butter until pink. When done baking, add shrimp to jambalaya. Cover and let stand 10 minutes to reheat shrimp.

4 to 6 servings

Shrimp and Rice

6	cups cooked rice	2	tablespoons juice from a jar of green olives
3	pounds cooked shrimp		
1½	cups chopped celery		Salt and pepper to taste
2	onions, chopped		
1	(16-ounce) bottle Thousand Island salad dressing	8	slices bacon, cut into 2-inch pieces and partially cooked
1	(8-ounce) can sliced water chestnuts, drained		

Preheat oven to 350 degrees.

Combine all ingredients except bacon and divide between two 11x14-inch glass casserole dishes. Arrange bacon on top. Bake 30 to 35 minutes or until bacon is crisp.

12 servings

Marinated Shrimp and Grits

Easy and Quick - and tastes really special.

Step One

1½	cups chicken broth	1	cup grated white or
1½	cups milk		yellow Cheddar
¾	cup quick-cooking grits		cheese
¼	teaspoon salt		

Step Two

1	cup diced raw bacon	½	cup thinly sliced red
1	package frozen		bell pepper strips
	marinated and grilled	½	cup slivered onion
	shrimp, slightly		Sliced green onion and
	thawed		grated cheese for
½	cup thinly sliced green		garnish
	bell pepper strips		

Bring broth and milk to a boil in a large saucepan. Stir in grits and salt and return to a boil. Cover and reduce heat to low. Cook 5 minutes or until thickened, stirring occasionally. Stir in cheese. Keep warm.

For second step, cook bacon in a skillet until crisp. Drain all but 2 tablespoons of bacon fat from skillet. Add shrimp, bell peppers and onion to bacon in skillet. Cook until vegetables are tender and shrimp is thoroughly heated, gently stirring occasionally.

Serve shrimp mixture over warm cheese grits. Garnish with green onion and grated cheese.

4 to 6 servings

Every year we used to gather at the grandparent's beach house where G'mama would educate us in the ways of the South - especially as it pertains to fresh local seafood and produce. The smell of the sea brings a gnawing hunger to me again for the good fresh fish and those happy days.

Seafood

Aunt Cynthia's Salmon Casserole

Great on a cool night, served with grits and sliced tomatoes!

1	(16-ounce) can pink salmon, undrained	2	(5-ounce) cans evaporated milk
8	saltine crackers, crushed		Black pepper to taste
4	tablespoons margarine, melted	1	teaspoon apple cider vinegar
1	medium onion, minced	¼	teaspoon Tabasco sauce

Preheat oven to 350 degrees. Spray a casserole dish with nonstick cooking spray.

Combine all ingredients. Pour mixture into prepared casserole dish. Bake 25 minutes or until lightly browned.

4 servings

Margarine can be omitted, if desired.

Charleston Shrimp Casserole

An easy, tasty meal

1	pound raw shrimp	1	teaspoon prepared mustard
2	quarts water		
1	tablespoon salt	⅛	teaspoon salt
32	saltine crackers, crushed	3	eggs, slightly beaten
2	cups milk	4	teaspoons bacon drippings

Cook shrimp in 2 quarts water and 1 tablespoon salt for 5 minutes. Drain and cool, then peel and devein. Combine shrimp, cracker crumbs and milk. Let stand 3 hours or more.

Preheat oven to 350 degrees.

Add mustard, ⅛ teaspoon salt and eggs and mix well. Pour mixture into a greased 2-quart casserole. Drizzle bacon drippings on top. Bake 1 hour.

4 servings

Wild Shrimp and Crab Rice

8 ounces fresh mushrooms, sliced
3 stalks celery, chopped
Butter for sautéing
1 (6-ounce) package wild rice, cooked
1 pound crabmeat
1 pound cooked and peeled shrimp
1 (10¾-ounce) can condensed cream of shrimp soup
2 tablespoons heavy cream
½ cup mayonnaise
Salt and pepper to taste

This recipe came to me from my wonderful sister. As the only girls out of five children, we have a special bond and thank God for her!

Preheat oven to 350 degrees.

Sauté mushrooms and celery in butter. Remove from heat and mix in rice, crabmeat and shrimp.

In a mixing bowl, combine soup, cream, mayonnaise, salt and pepper. Stir into seafood mixture and mix thoroughly. Transfer to a baking dish. Bake, uncovered, for 30 minutes.

8 servings

Seafood Casserole

¾ cup butter
1 pound or more cooked lobster, cut into large cubes
1 pound raw medium shrimp
1 pound scallops, patted dry, halved if large
1½ teaspoons dry mustard
12-15 tablespoons flour
15 slices firm white bread, crusts removed
1½ quarts cream
Salt to taste
Paprika to taste
½ cup sherry, or ¼ cup sherry and ¼ cup brandy
Butter crackers, crushed and mixed with melted butter

Preheat oven to 325 degrees.

Melt butter in a large skillet. Add lobster, shrimp and scallops and sauté 5 minutes or until tender. Sprinkle with mustard and flour. Add as much cream as skillet can hold. Cook and stir until mixture thickens.

Place bread slices in a large bowl. Add remaining cream. Stir in seafood mixture. Season with salt and paprika. Mix in sherry.

Transfer mixture to a greased large, shallow baking dish. Spread buttered cracker crumbs over casserole. Bake 40 to 45 minutes.

12 to 15 servings

Seafood

Aunt Edna Aimar's Deviled Crabmeat on a Platter

½ cup butter
1 medium onion, chopped
1 large bay leaf, finely minced
1 dash ground thyme
1 pound fresh white crabmeat, checked over for shell

2 hard-cooked eggs, chopped
Salt and pepper to taste
White cracker crumbs
Butter

Melt butter in a skillet. Add onion, bay leaf and thyme and sauté. Add crabmeat and eggs. Season with salt and pepper. Cook until light golden but not browned. Arrange on an ovenproof platter. Sprinkle with cracker crumbs and dot with butter. Refrigerate until ready to cook.

When ready to bake, preheat oven to 350 degrees. Bake 20 minutes or until cracker crumbs brown. Serve hot.

4 to 6 servings

Deviled Crabs
"Heavenly"

½ cup butter
½ cup chopped celery
½ cup chopped onion
2 slices bread, toasted
¼ cup sherry
Dash of hot pepper sauce

1 pound lump crabmeat or backfin
1½ tablespoons lemon juice
Bread crumbs
Dash of paprika

Preheat oven to 350 degrees.

Melt butter in a saucepan over low heat. Add celery and onion and cook 5 minutes. Break toasted bread into dime-size pieces and fold into vegetable mixture. Stir in sherry and hot sauce.

Sprinkle crabmeat with lemon juice. Gently fold crab into vegetable mixture. Spoon mixture into 8 to 10 crab tins. Sprinkle with bread crumbs and paprika. Bake 15 minutes.

8 to 10 servings

Pentagon Shrimp Creole

1	cup vegetable oil, or ½ cup oil and ½ cup bacon drippings		1	teaspoon curry powder
2	cups diced celery		1	teaspoon salt
1	cup chopped celery leaves		1	teaspoon black pepper
2	cups sliced or chopped green bell pepper		1	teaspoon cayenne pepper
5	cups sliced or chopped onion		3	large bay leaves
1	cup chili sauce		8	ounces (about 1⅔ cups) blanched almonds, chopped and toasted
1	cup raisins		2	(28-ounce) cans tomatoes, chopped
1	teaspoon thyme		3-5	pounds cooked and peeled shrimp

Heat oil in a large skillet or roasting pan. Add celery, celery leaves, bell pepper and onion and cook over low heat until onion is transparent but not brown. Add chili sauce, raisins, thyme, curry powder, salt, black pepper, cayenne pepper, bay leaves, almonds and tomatoes. Simmer gently for 1 hour, stirring occasionally.

Add shrimp and cook 1 hour longer. Serve over rice.

20 servings

For best flavor, prepare the sauce early in the day and refrigerate to allow flavors to blend.

This is an unusual and delicious version of our Southern Creole dishes.
I got the recipe from Mrs. Lu Poggemeyer at Camp Lejune Marine Base, North Carolina. She got the recipe while her husband was serving at the Pentagon in Washington, D.C. The recipe was enlarged to satisfy Marine appetites; but since the sauce is easily frozen, it can be brought out as needed for smaller dinners.

Granny's Shrimp Newberg
A family favorite

4	tablespoons butter or margarine		½	cup ketchup
3½	tablespoons all-purpose flour		1½	tablespoons Worcestershire sauce
2	cups whole milk		1	pound cooked and peeled shrimp

Melt butter in a heavy saucepan. Add flour and stir until bubbly. Gradually whisk in milk until smooth. Blend in ketchup and Worcestershire sauce. Add shrimp just before serving.

2 or 3 servings

Seafood

Steamed Mussels in Garlic and Butter

4	pounds Maine mussels	1	tablespoon chopped garlic
2	quarts water	1	tablespoon fresh or dried parsley
½	cup light butter		
1	tablespoon salt	1	loaf Italian bread or French baguette, sliced
2	heaping tablespoons Romano cheese		

Clean mussels using a scrub brush, removing beards.

Combine water, butter, salt, cheese, garlic and parsley in large stockpot. Bring to a boil. Add mussels. Reduce heat and cover. Simmer, checking frequently, 10 to 15 minutes or until shells open.

Spoon mussels into individual serving bowls. Ladle broth over mussels. Serve bread on the side to be dipped in the broth or in seasoned olive oil.

4 or 5 servings

Bliss Deviled Crab

1	pound lump crabmeat	½	teaspoon black pepper
2	eggs, beaten	2	cups dry stuffing mix, crushed fine
¼	cup bread crumbs		
1	teaspoon salt	½	cup butter

Preheat oven to 375 degrees.

Mix crabmeat, eggs, bread crumbs, salt and pepper. Spoon into devil crab shells. Top with stuffing mix and drizzle with butter. Bake 15 minutes or until topping is browned.

8 servings

Seafood

Soft Seafood Tacos Delight

Batter

1	cup plus 2 tablespoons beer (not dark)	1	teaspoon dry mustard
1	cup flour	1	teaspoon dried oregano
1½	teaspoons salt	½	teaspoon dried cilantro
1	teaspoon garlic powder	½	teaspoon black pepper

Sauce

⅓	cup mayonnaise	½	tablespoon fresh lime
⅓	cup yogurt		juice
½	teaspoon sea salt		

Taco and Filling

1	pound firm white fish, such as cod or grouper, or 2 pounds medium shrimp, peeled	2	quarts vegetable or canola oil
			Sea salt
	Flour for dredging	12	corn tortillas
		2	limes, cut into wedges
		½	head iceberg lettuce, shredded

Blend all batter ingredients in a food processor or blender for 30 seconds or until smooth. Pour into a bowl and let stand 1 hour.

Combine all sauce ingredients. Cover and chill until ready to use.

If using fish, cut into 3-x½-inch strips. Dredge seafood in flour. Knock off excess and then coat in batter. Fry in 2 inches of oil heated to 350 degrees in a 4-quart saucepan. Cook in batches, stirring seafood around, 2 to 3 minutes for fish, 1 to 2 minutes for shrimp or until batter is pale golden. Remove seafood from oil and drain. When all batches are cooked, wait about 5 to 10 minutes. Fry batches again until batter is golden brown. Drain and sprinkle with sea salt.

Wrap tortillas in plastic and heat in a microwave for 20 seconds. To assemble tacos, place seafood down the middle of each tortilla. Top with sauce and a squeeze of lime juice. Add lettuce and fold over.

4 to 6 servings

This can be served with homemade guacamole and salsa. However, the tacos are so good that often in our house, we never use these condiments.

Seafood

Miss Julie's Shrimp Pie

I love to use small creek shrimp in this recipe. We often catch them in the tidal creek behind our house. Everyone was delighted when I used to add fresh picked crab to the filling.

2 tablespoons chopped onion
⅓ cup chopped green bell pepper
4 tablespoons butter
2 cups cooked and peeled shrimp
1 cup condensed cream of mushroom soup
½ cup milk
1 tablespoon ketchup
1 tablespoon Worcestershire sauce
Salt and pepper to taste
1 double-crust pie shell

Preheat oven to 400 degrees.

Sauté onion and bell pepper in butter. Stir in shrimp, soup, milk, ketchup and Worcestershire sauce. Season with salt and pepper.

Place bottom crust in pie pan and bake about 2 minutes. Pour shrimp mixture into hot crust and cover with top crust. Cut slits in top to allow steam to escape.

Reduce heat to 350 degrees and bake for 20 minutes or until crust is light brown. Remove carefully from oven as filling will be very "soupy". Cool for a few minutes before serving.

4 to 6 servings

Oyster Pie

2 pints oysters plus ¼ cup of juice
Salt and pepper to taste (lots of pepper)
2 cups crushed cracker crumbs
½ cup margarine or butter, melted
¼ cup Worcestershire sauce
1 cup half-and-half
½ teaspoon salt

Preheat oven to 350 degrees.

Season oysters with salt and pepper. Combine cracker crumbs with butter.

Place a third of buttered crumbs in the bottom of a greased pie dish. Add half the oysters. Repeat layers, ending with crumbs.

Mix together Worcestershire sauce, half-and-half and salt. Pour over layers. Bake 40 minutes.

8 servings

Helen's Rockville Shrimp Pie

1	large onion, chopped	1½	cups grated sharp Cheddar cheese
1	large green bell pepper, chopped	1½	pounds cooked and peeled shrimp
3	stalks celery, chopped	8	drops Tabasco sauce
½	cup margarine or butter	1	tablespoon Worcestershire sauce
1	(14½-ounce) can crushed tomatoes (2 cups)	1	teaspoon salt
		1	teaspoon black pepper
4	slices white bread, crumbled	1	teaspoon sugar
		½	cup grated sharp Cheddar cheese

This recipe originally came from one of the Gullah cooks at the Rockville Race House Party.

Preheat oven to 350 degrees.

Sauté onion, bell pepper and celery in margarine. Process tomatoes and crumbled bread in a blender.

Add sautéed vegetables to tomato mixture in a bowl. Stir in 1½ cups cheese, shrimp, Tabasco sauce, Worcestershire sauce, salt, black pepper and sugar.

Pour mixture into a greased 1½-quart casserole dish. Sprinkle with ½ cup cheese. Bake 30 minutes or until bubbling.

8 servings

Lowcountry Oyster Pie

1	sleeve saltine crackers		Salt and pepper to taste
1	pat butter	4	ounces Cheddar cheese, grated
3	pints oysters		
	Heavy cream		

Remember: oysters are only in season in the months that contain the letter "R". (September, October, November, December, January, February, March, and April)

Preheat oven to 350 degrees.

Crumble most of saltine crackers into the bottom of a casserole dish. Dot with butter.

Drain oysters slightly and place on crackers in dish. Add enough cream to thicken mixture without making it soggy. Season with salt and pepper. Top with remaining cracker crumbs, then with cheese. Bake 30 minutes.

8 servings

Seafood

Oysters Rockefeller Casserole

2	tablespoons butter	1	cup saltine or butter cracker crumbs
2	(10-ounce) packages frozen chopped spinach, thawed and drained	2	cloves garlic, minced
		6	crackers
		3	quarts oysters, drained
1	tablespoon lemon juice	¼	cup Parmesan cheese
1	tablespoon Worcestershire sauce	1	(12-ounce) package grated Cheddar cheese
	Black pepper to taste		
	Hot pepper sauce to taste	1	(12-ounce) package grated mozzarella cheese
4	tablespoons butter		
½	medium onion, grated		

Preheat oven to 350 degrees.

Heat 2 tablespoons butter over medium heat. Add spinach and stir until excess butter evaporates. Mix in lemon juice, Worcestershire sauce, black pepper and pepper sauce.

In a mixing bowl, combine 4 tablespoons butter, onion, cracker crumbs and garlic. Mix in spinach mixture.

Crumble 6 crackers over the bottom of a greased shallow baking dish. Layer spinach mixture, oysters and cheeses, ending with layers of cheeses. Bake 45 minutes. Serve immediately.

8 to 12 servings

Oysters Corley

1	(10-ounce) package frozen spinach		Salt and pepper to taste
			Tabasco sauce to taste
2	tablespoons butter, softened	12	raw oysters
		2	tablespoons butter
2	tablespoons sour cream	½	teaspoon samson sauce
1	teaspoon lemon juice		

Cook spinach until barely tender. Drain well. Mix in 2 tablespoons softened butter, sour cream, lemon juice, salt, pepper and Tabasco sauce. Spoon mixture into 4 ramekins.

Place 3 oysters on each spinach mound. Dot with remaining butter and season with samson sauce. Broil until heated through and oysters begin to curl.

4 servings

Crab Quiche

½	cup mayonnaise	8	ounces Swiss cheese, cut into cubes
2	tablespoons flour	⅓	cup chopped green onions
2	eggs, beaten		
½	cup milk	1	(9-inch) pie crust, unbaked
1	(6-ounce) can crabmeat, drained		Parsley for garnish

Preheat oven to 350 degrees.

Combine mayonnaise, flour, eggs and milk. Mix well. Stir in crabmeat, cheese and onions. Pour into pie crust.

Bake 30 to 40 minutes. Garnish with parsley and bake 10 minutes longer.

4 to 6 servings

Bitsy Aimar's Salmon Shells

2	tablespoons butter	½	cup minced fresh parsley
⅓	cup flour		
1	cup whole milk	½	medium onion, minced
1	teaspoon dry mustard	1½	tablespoons butter
1	teaspoon Worcestershire sauce	1	(16-ounce) can sockeye salmon
	Salt to taste	12-14	saltine crackers, crushed
		1	tablespoon butter

Melt 2 tablespoons butter in a saucepan over medium heat. Mix in flour until smooth. Whisk in milk. Cook and stir until sauce is thickened. Add mustard, Worcestershire sauce, salt and parsley. Sauté onion in 1½ tablespoons butter until browned and add to sauce.

Drain and remove bones and skin from salmon. Break salmon into chunks and add to sauce. Spoon mixture into flat (beach-type) 5½-inch wide shells.

Preheat oven to 350 degrees.

Sauté cracker crumbs in 1 tablespoon butter until golden brown. Sprinkle crumbs over mixture in shells. Place shells on a baking sheet. Bake until thoroughly heated, but do not boil.

4 servings

Seafood

Crabmeat Divan

1	(10-ounce) package frozen broccoli stalks	½	teaspoon prepared mustard
1	(6-ounce) can crabmeat, drained	1	teaspoon grated onion
⅓	cup mayonnaise	¼	cup grated processed cheese
1½	teaspoons lemon juice		

Preheat oven to 350 degrees.

Cook broccoli and drain. Arrange in a rectangular casserole dish with the florets facing outward. Place the crabmeat in the middle of the dish on top the broccoli stems.

Mix mayonnaise, lemon juice, mustard and onion and spoon over crabmeat. Top with cheese. Bake 20 minutes.

4 servings

Linda's Seafood Pastry

This recipe treats people special and makes you a gourmet.

1	(8-count) can crescent rolls		Oil for sautéing
3-4	green onions, green tips reserved for garnish	12	large sea scallops
			Fresh lemon juice
			Fontina cheese, grated
2-3	cloves garlic, minced	1	egg yolk, beaten

Preheat oven to 350 degrees.

Pinch two crescent rolls together with fingers to form a square pastry shell. Repeat with remaining rolls. Place each shell in a 4x6-inch baking dish. Refrigerate dough until ready to use to prevent tearing.

Sauté onions and garlic in oil until lightly browned. Add scallops and a squeeze of lemon juice and sauté 2 minutes. Cool slightly.

Cover pastry shell with grated cheese, using as much as desired. Place 3 scallops with some of garlic and onion mixture on each pastry. Pinch corners of pastry together at the seams to seal. Brush lightly with egg yolk. Sprinkle a bit more cheese over the top. Bake 10 to 13 minutes or until browned. During last 3 minutes of baking, garnish with green onion tips cut with scissors. Serve immediately.

4 servings

Seafood

Pine Bark Fish Stew

8	ounces fat back or salt pork	2	dashes Tabasco sauce
6	medium onions, finely chopped	1	tablespoon dried or fresh parsley
3	medium cloves garlic, finely chopped	½	teaspoon rosemary (optional)
1	(32-ounce) bottle ketchup		Cayenne pepper to taste (use more than you think you should)
2	(28-ounce) cans tomatoes		Salt to taste
3	(6-ounce) cans tomato paste	2-4	cups water
3	tablespoons Worcestershire sauce	12	medium fish or 4 pounds fish fillets

This recipe is a favorite one-dish meal served in the "Pee Dee" area of South Carolina. The "Pine Bark" comes from the fact that it was cooked in an old iron wash pot over a fire made from slabs of pine bark.

Slice fat back and fry until crisp in a large heavy Dutch oven. Remove crisp pork and set aside, reserving drippings in pan. Add onions and garlic and sauté until transparent. Add ketchup, tomatoes, tomato paste, Worcestershire sauce, Tabasco sauce, parsley, rosemary, cayenne pepper and salt. Add enough water to give mixture a soupy consistency. Cover and cook over low heat for at least 1 hour. Add fish 30 minutes before serving. Serve in soup bowls over cooked rice.

12 servings

Allow one medium fish or one-third pound of fillet per person. The best kind to use is any fresh-water broad fish or salt-water perch or flounder.

Crabmeat in Shells

2	cups crabmeat	½	teaspoon salt
4	tablespoons butter	¼	teaspoon basil
½	cup cream	¼	teaspoon thyme
2	tablespoons chopped onion		Small scallop sea shells baking pastry
	Zest of ¼ lemon		Bread crumbs
3	tablespoons chopped parsley		Parmesan cheese

Preheat oven to 400 degrees.

Combine crabmeat, butter, cream, onion, zest, parsley, salt, basil and thyme. Spoon mixture into shells. Top with bread crumbs and cheese. Bake 10 to 15 minutes.

Shrimp and Grits

When I was a child, my family spent summers at Pawleys Island, where, when the tide was right, on some hot, boring afternoon all of the cousins would pick up the ancient seine net. I, being the oldest, would oversee the shrimping. Even with seven pairs of scrawny arms and tiny hands, it took forever to haul in our catch of creek shrimp. (I guess we must have either had some help from the adults in the house or somebody went to Lachicotte's and bought some more shrimp or we'd still be there!) Tired and sore, we wondered if the pain was worth the reward. Then Aunt Molly would boil the little shrimp, and we'd peel them, popping them in our mouths after dipping them in pots of melted butter on the back porch while we watched the sun set over the creek. Our backs ached from casting the net, our faces were greasy with sweet butter, and my grandmother kept us in stitches with stories we'd heard a hundred times before as the light faded, revealing the summer night sky. Sound magical? Idyllic? It was nothing compared to what happened the next morning and the real reason we went to the trouble of catching those shrimp.

We knew those leftover shrimp would wind up sizzling in an old cast iron skillet, tossed with a little butter and mounded onto a heaping plateful of grits. Now these grits were not of the tasteless instant variety, no. We're talking about stone ground whole grain yellow grits that you had to soak overnight in "beach water" and cook for hours over a low flame, constantly adding more milk and butter until the consistency was silken and big buttery bubbles popped on the surface. Fat slices of summer tomatoes and crisp bacon turned breakfast into a "break-feast!"

At the time, I know we children thought we were the only people on earth who had ever thought of such a thing. It was our family secret, my mama's invention, this concoction of just caught shrimp with the slightly metallic taste of the sea and creamy golden grits so rich it seemed like it must be a sin to eat it.

Desserts

"Manna from Heaven"

Steeple of Light

Rising a graceful 186 feet above the skyline
of Charleston, St Michael's steeple is a beacon to all.
As we look first onto the rooftops, then out into the
harbor and on past to the sea, the timeless vastness
of God's creation is apparent. As St. Michael's moves
from its first 250 years to the future and
Christ's coming again in glory, we rejoice with
praise and thanksgiving to the Almighty in
all his infinite power. Glory to God!

"And after these things I heard a great
voice of much people in heaven, saying, Alleluia;
Salvation and glory and honor and power unto
the Lord our God."
Revelation 19:1

Tearoom Lemon Cake

Easy, Beautiful and Delicious

1	(18½-ounce) package yellow cake mix	1	tablespoon lemon zest
½	cup butter, softened	1	teaspoon vanilla
6	eggs	¾	cup raspberry preserves
½	cup heavy cream	1½	cups sliced almonds, toasted
½	cup water		

Lemon Frosting

3	(8-ounce) packages cream cheese, softened	1	cup powdered sugar
		3	tablespoons fresh lemon juice
1	(11¾-ounce) jar lemon curd	1	tablespoon lemon zest

Preheat oven to 350 degrees.

Grease 2 (9-inch) springform pans with 2¾-inch sides.

Combine cake mix, butter, eggs, cream, water, lemon zest and vanilla. Beat about 2 minutes or until smooth. Divide batter between the prepared pans. Bake 25 to 30 minutes or until a toothpick inserted in the center comes out clean. Cool thoroughly on racks. After cooling, cut around side of pans to loosen, release sides and remove cakes. Cut each cake in half horizontally, resulting in 4 layers.

Place one layer, cut-side up, on a cake plate. Spread with ¼ cup preserves, then ¾ cup frosting. Repeat layers twice. Top with final cake layer, cut-side down. Frost sides and top with remaining frosting. Press almonds into sides of cake and chill at least 2 hours or until frosting sets.

To make frosting, cream together all ingredients until smooth.

This cake was served one year at the Christian Family Y tearoom, manned by lots of St. Michaelites and other church members to raise funds for the Y. It was an instant hit and the recipe has been shared by many.

Desserts

195

Beverly's
Chocolate Pound Cake

1 cup butter, softened	½ teaspoon salt
½ cup vegetable shortening	½ cup cocoa powder
3 cups sugar	1 teaspoon baking powder
5 eggs	1¼ cups milk
3 cups flour	1 tablespoon vanilla

Icing

5½ tablespoons butter or margarine	¼ cup cocoa powder
⅓ cup milk	1 (1-pound) box powdered sugar

Preheat oven to 325 degrees.

Cream butter, shortening and sugar. Add eggs, one at a time, beating well after each addition. Sift together flour, salt, cocoa powder and baking powder. Mix dry ingredients into creamed mixture alternately with milk. Mix in vanilla. Beat well. Pour batter into a lightly greased and floured tube pan and bake 1 hour, 15 minutes or until a straw inserted in the center comes out clean.

To make icing, heat butter, milk and cocoa powder in a medium saucepan over low heat. Remove from heat and mix in powdered sugar until smooth. Add extra milk if needed. Pour icing over cake. Add any leftover icing to the center hole in the cake.

Omit cocoa powder and this makes a wonderful pound cake. Bake at 300 degrees for 1½ hours. Be careful not to overbeat batter. Stir in dry ingredients and milk by hand, then beat with mixer for 30 seconds before pouring into pan.

Desserts

Grandmama Lucy's Lavender Cake

3 cups cake flour
1½ teaspoons baking powder
1 teaspoon baking soda
½ teaspoon salt
1 cup unsalted butter
1½ cups granulated sugar
1 tablespoon dried lavender flowers
4 eggs, beaten
½ teaspoon lemon extract
1 teaspoon vanilla
1 cup plain yogurt
1 teaspoon finely grated lemon zest
2 tablespoons honey
½ cup sifted powdered sugar
1 teaspoon lemon juice

Preheat oven to 325 degrees.

Sift together flour, baking powder, baking soda and salt onto wax paper.

Cream butter. Add granulated sugar and lavender and beat well. Mix in eggs, lemon extract and vanilla. Slowly beat in dry ingredients. Add yogurt and lemon zest. Spoon batter into a greased Bundt pan. Bake 55 to 60 minutes.

Cool 1 hour on a rack. Combine honey, powdered sugar and lemon juice in a small saucepan. Heat and pour over cooled cake. Dust with extra powdered sugar.

How sweet are your words to my taste, sweeter than honey to my mouth.

~ Psalm 119:103

Desserts

The Lady Irene Charleston Cake

I have been making this cake for 20 years. It was originally the Lady Baltimore recipe but I've changed it to suit myself. What really makes it special is the layer of filling in the middle - made with the leftover wine used to soak the fruit. The first time I made this cake was for the St. Michael's bazaar and have made it every year since. Sometimes people fight over who gets to purchase the cake (not really fight but there's always a mad dash to get to it first).

Sometimes I'll make this as a special gift for special people.

Original Version

½ cup butter, softened	½ teaspoon salt
2 cups sugar	1 cup milk
4 jumbo eggs	1 teaspoon vanilla
3 cups flour	1 teaspoon almond
1 tablespoon baking	extract
powder	½ cup sherry

Preheat oven to 350 degrees.

Cream butter and sugar well. Add eggs and beat well. Sift together flour, baking powder and salt (or use 3 cups self-rising flour). Mix dry ingredients into creamed mixture alternately with milk. Add vanilla and almond extract. Pour batter into three greased 9-inch round cake pans. Bake 30 minutes or until slightly browned on top and a toothpick inserted in the center comes out clean. Remove from oven and turn upside down on a serving plate. While hot, pour sherry over layers. Cool.

Modern Version

1 (18½-ounce) package	1 teaspoon vanilla
yellow cake mix	2 teaspoons almond
¾ cup water	extract
½ cup sherry	½ cup sherry
⅓ cup vegetable oil	

Preheat oven to 350 degrees.

Pour cake mix into a large mixing bowl. Add water, oil, vanilla and almond extract. Mix on low speed. Pour into a greased Bundt pan.

Bake 40 minutes or until a toothpick inserted in the cake comes out clean. Do not overcook or overbrown. When cool, slice into 3 layers and pour sherry over the layers.

Icing

1½ cups raisins	3 jumbo egg whites
1½ cups coarsely chopped	1½ cups sugar
pecans	¼ cup water
2 (10-ounce) jars	1 teaspoon vanilla
maraschino cherries,	2 teaspoons almond
halved	extract
3½ cups sherry	

Sauce

¾ cup orange juice
1 cup sugar

4 heaping tablespoons cornstarch dissolved in a small amount of water

For icing, layer raisins, pecans and cherries in order listed in a bowl. Pour sherry over layers. Cover and let stand overnight. In the morning, drain, reserving liquid for sauce. Place egg whites, sugar, water, vanilla and almond extract in the top of a double boiler. Beat with an electric mixer on high speed over gently boiling water until icing is spreadable. Mix in drained fruit and nuts.

Prepare sauce by combining reserved liquid, orange juice, sugar and cornstarch in a saucepan. Cook over medium heat until thickened and clear. Cool.

Spread sauce on each cake layer. Frost each layer with fruited icing. Stack layers and frost top and sides of cake.

Thelma Aimar's Coconut Layer Cake

Cake

1	cup unsalted butter, softened
2	cups sugar
4	eggs, separated
2	cups self-rising flour

1	cup all-purpose flour
1	teaspoon baking powder
1	cup whole milk
2	teaspoons vanilla

Icing

2	cups sugar
5	tablespoons water
4	egg whites

1	tablespoon cream of tartar
2	tablespoons vanilla

Decorations

1	coconut, peeled and finely grated
1	(15-ounce) can crushed pineapple, drained

Pecan halves or maraschino cherries (optional)

Preheat oven to 350 degrees.

Cream butter, sugar and egg yolks together.

Stir together flours and baking powder. Beat egg whites until stiff. Add dry ingredients and milk alternately to creamed mixture. Fold in egg whites and vanilla.

Divide batter among 4 greased and floured 9-inch round cake pans. Bake until cake separates from sides of pans and springs back in the center. Cool on wire racks.

To make icing, bring water in the bottom of a double boiler to a boil. Add all icing ingredients except vanilla to top of double boiler. Beat with an electric mixer for 7 to 8 minutes or until peaks form. Remove from stove but keep in double boiler. Stir in vanilla.

To assemble cake, ice first layer. Sprinkle with coconut and pineapple. Top with second layer. Repeat icing process with remaining layers. Garnish icing on top layer with pecan halves or cherries.

Apple Cake

1	cup vegetable oil	1	teaspoon vanilla
2	cups sugar	1	cup pecans or walnuts
3	eggs	½	cup raisins
2	cups self-rising flour	1	teaspoon cinnamon
3	cups chopped apple	1	teaspoon nutmeg

Delicious served with whipped cream or vanilla ice cream.

Preheat oven to 350 degrees.

Beat together oil, sugar and eggs. Add flour and beat thoroughly. Mix in apple, vanilla, pecans, raisins, cinnamon and nutmeg until well blended.

Pour into a greased and floured 11x7-inch or 8-inch square baking pan. Bake 40 to 45 minutes.

12 or more servings

Apple Spice Cake

3	eggs	¼	teaspoon salt
3	tablespoons milk	¾	cup sugar
1	teaspoon vanilla	¾	cup vegetable oil or melted butter
2	teaspoon cinnamon		
½	teaspoon nutmeg	2	baking apples, peeled and diced
1½	cups all-purpose flour		
1	teaspoon baking powder		

Preheat oven to 350 degrees.

Beat together eggs, milk and vanilla. Sift cinnamon, nutmeg, flour, baking powder, salt and sugar together. Mix dry ingredients into egg mixture alternately with oil. Fold in apple.

Pour batter into a greased and floured loaf pan. Bake 55 minutes.

Hummingbird Cake

I created this recipe for my husband's 34th birthday at our family farm, Dawhoo. I remember it was a beautiful spring day with the wildflowers and new grasses just rearing their heads and azaleas blooming in profusion under moss-laden oaks.

Cake

3	cups all-purpose flour	1½	teaspoons vanilla
1½	cups vegetable oil	1	(8-ounce) can crushed pineapple, undrained
3	eggs, beaten		
2	cups sugar	2	cups diced banana
1	teaspoon salt	¾	cup chopped pecans
1	teaspoon baking soda	¼	cup chopped walnuts
1	teaspoon cinnamon		

Icing

1	cup cream cheese, softened	4	tablespoons butter
		1½	teaspoons vanilla
1	(1-pound) box powdered sugar		Pinch of salt
		1	cup chopped pecans

Preheat oven to 350 degrees.

Mix all cake ingredients together by hand. Pour batter into two greased and floured 9-inch round cake pans. Bake 45 to 50 minutes. Do not overbake.

To make icing, mix all ingredients except pecans using an electric mixer. Fold in pecans. Frost between layers and on outside of cake.

8 servings

Sour Cream Pound Cake

1½	cups butter	3	cups sifted all-purpose flour
2	cups sugar		
6	eggs, separated	¼	teaspoon baking soda
1	cup sour cream	1½	teaspoons vanilla

Preheat oven to 300 degrees.

Cream butter, sugar and egg yolks. Beat well. Mix in sour cream, flour and baking soda.

Beat egg whites until stiff. Fold egg whites into batter. Add vanilla. Pour batter into a greased and floured tube pan. Bake 1½ hours.

Planters Punch Cake

¾	cup butter	1	(14-ounce) can sweetened condensed milk
1	(18½-ounce) package yellow cake mix		
1	(20-ounce) can crushed pineapple, drained	1	(8-ounce) package cream cheese, softened
1	(26-ounce) jar mango spears, drained and chopped	2	eggs
		1	cup chopped pecans
½	cup dark rum	2	cups heavy cream, whipped, or frozen whipped topping

Preheat oven to 350 degrees.

Cut butter into cake mix with a pastry cutter. Set aside 1½ cups of mixture. Press remainder into a 9x13-inch baking pan. Layer pineapple and mango over crust. Drizzle with half the rum.

Combine remaining rum, condensed milk, cream cheese and eggs in a mixing bowl. Beat on medium speed until smooth. Pour over fruit. Sprinkle with reserved cake crumb mixture and pecans.

Bake 50 to 55 minutes or until set and slightly browned. Chill 8 hours. Top with whipped cream.

Cream Cheese Pound Cake

1½	cups butter or margarine, softened	6	eggs
		3	cups all-purpose flour
1	(8-ounce) package cream cheese, softened	2	teaspoons vanilla extract
3	cups sugar	1	tablespoon almond extract

Cream butter and cream cheese in a large mixing bowl. Add sugar. Beat in eggs, one at a time, until blended. Sift flour 3 times and add to batter. Blend well. Mix in extracts.

Pour batter into a greased and floured 12-cup Bundt pan. Place pan in cold oven. Turn oven to 300 degrees and bake 1½ to 2 hours or until a toothpick inserted in the center comes out clean.

Carrot Cake

4	eggs	1	teaspoon baking soda
1½	cups vegetable oil	2	teaspoons cinnamon
2	cups sugar	¼	teaspoon salt
2	cups flour	3	cups grated carrot
1	teaspoon baking powder		

Carrot Cake Icing

1	(8-ounce) package cream cheese, softened	1	(16-ounce) box powdered sugar
½	cup butter, softened	1	teaspoon vanilla
		1	cup chopped pecans

Preheat oven to 375 degrees.

Blend together eggs and oil. Sift together sugar, flour, baking powder, baking soda, cinnamon and salt. Mix dry ingredients into oil mixture. Add carrot and blend well. Pour batter into two greased and floured 9-inch round cake pans. Bake 30 to 40 minutes. Cool.

To make icing, cream together cream cheese and butter. Add sugar, vanilla and pecans. Mix well. Spread icing between layers and on outside of cake.

Grandmother's Pumpkin Pie

This 70 year old recipe works!

My husband would not eat pumpkin pie - then he tasted this and now he's hooked.

2	eggs, lightly beaten	¼	teaspoon ground cloves
1	(16-ounce) can pumpkin	1	cup heavy cream
¾	cup sugar	⅔	cup bourbon
½	teaspoon salt	1	(9-inch) pie crust, unbaked
1	teaspoon cinnamon		
½	teaspoon ground ginger		

Preheat oven to 425 degrees.

Combine eggs and pumpkin in a mixing bowl. Mix sugar, salt, cinnamon, ginger and cloves and add to pumpkin mixture. Blend in cream and bourbon. Mix thoroughly.

Pour filling into pie crust. Bake 15 minutes. Reduce heat to 350 degrees and bake 45 to 50 minutes longer.

6 to 8 servings

Chocolate Cake

No eggs or butter

Cake

2	cups cake flour	1	cup water
1	cup sugar	1	cup mayonnaise
4	heaping tablespoons cocoa powder	2	tablespoons blackberry jelly
1	teaspoon baking soda	1	tablespoon vanilla
¼	teaspoon salt		

Icing

2	(1-ounce) squares unsweetened baking chocolate	1	(14-ounce) can sweetened condensed milk
2	tablespoons butter Dash of salt	1	tablespoon vanilla

Preheat oven to 325 degrees.

Sift together flour, sugar, cocoa powder, baking soda and salt in a bowl. Add water, mayonnaise, jelly and vanilla. Mix well. Batter will be thin. Pour into a greased 10x6-inch glass dish. Bake until a toothpick inserted in the center comes out clean. Cool.

To make icing, heat chocolate, butter and salt over medium heat until melted. Add milk. Cook and stir until mixture thickens. Stir in vanilla. Spread over cooled cake.

Amazing Coconut Pie

Easy and Delicious

2	cups milk	¼	cup butter or margarine
¾	cup sugar	1½	teaspoons vanilla
½	cup biscuit baking mix	1	cup flaked coconut
4	eggs		

Preheat oven to 350 degrees.

Combine milk, sugar, baking mix, eggs, butter and vanilla in a blender. Blend on low speed for 3 minutes. Pour mixture into an ungreased 9-inch pie pan. Let stand about 5 minutes. Sprinkle with coconut. Bake 40 minutes. Serve warm or cold.

8 servings

Desserts

Apple Pie with Crumble Crust Topping

6	medium apples such as Granny Smith	1	teaspoon nutmeg or to taste
	Lemon juice	1	frozen pie crust, unbaked
¾	cup granulated sugar		
½	cup brown sugar	2-3	tablespoons butter
1	teaspoon cinnamon or to taste		

Topping

1	(11-ounce) package pie crust mix	1	teaspoon cinnamon
¼	cup brown sugar or to taste	½-1	teaspoon nutmeg
			Water

Preheat oven to 350 degrees.

Peel and core apples and cut into bite-size pieces. Sprinkle apples with lemon juice as they are cut.

Mix sugars, cinnamon and nutmeg. Pour mixture over apples and toss. Dump apple mixture into pie crust. Dot with butter.

To prepare topping, combine dry pie crust mix, brown sugar, cinnamon and nutmeg. Add a small amount of water and cut in with a knife until mixture forms small clumps. Sprinkle topping over pie. Bake 45 to 50 minutes.

8 servings

Southern Peach Pie

5	cups peeled and sliced fresh peaches	1	cup sugar
1	pie crust, unbaked	⅓	cup flour
5	tablespoons butter or margarine, melted	1	egg
			Almond extract (optional)

Preheat oven to 350 degrees.

Place peach slices in pie crust. Combine butter, sugar, flour, egg and almond extract. Pour mixture over peaches. Bake 1 hour, 10 minutes.

8 servings

Jeanny's Pie Crust

Flaky as they come

2	cups all-purpose flour, unsifted	¼	cup cold milk
½	cup vegetable oil	1½	teaspoons salt

Place flour in a mixing bowl. Pour oil and milk at the same time into flour. Stir with a fork until mixed. Dough will look moist but should not be sticky. Form into a ball and cut in half.

Place one half between 2 (12-inch) square sheets of wax paper. Roll out dough gently to edges of paper. Dampen table to prevent paper from slipping. Peel off top paper. If dough tears, mend without moistening.

Lift bottom paper with crust by the top corners. Invert, paper-side up, onto a pie pan. Remove paper, add filling and trim crust.

Repeat for second half of dough. Place crust over filling. Trim top crust to rim of pan. Seal crusts with a fork or by fluting edge. Cut 3 or 4 slits near center to allow steam to escape.

Bake until golden brown, using time and temperature of individual pie recipe.

If only one crust is needed, freeze second crust for later use.

This recipe is unbelievably easy and so useful. Use it for fruit pies, meat pies, quiches - the possibilities are limited only by the cook's creativity. It's easier than buying ready-made and much tastier.

Fresh Fruit Cobbler

½	cup butter or margarine	4	cups fresh fruit, such as blueberries, blackberries or peaches, sweetened to taste if desired
1	cup sugar		
1	cup flour		
1	cup milk		
1	tablespoon baking powder		

Preheat oven to 375 degrees.

While oven heats, melt butter in a deep baking dish large enough to allow for cobbler to rise as it bakes.

Combine sugar, flour, milk and baking powder. Mix well. Pour batter over hot, melted butter. Pour fresh fruit over batter. Bake 25 to 30 minutes or until brown and bubbly.

Desserts

Brandy Alexander Pie

1	envelope unflavored gelatin	⅓	cup sugar
½	cup cold water	1	cup heavy cream, whipped
⅓	cup sugar	1	graham cracker crust (optional)
⅛	teaspoon salt		Shaved chocolate curls for garnish
3	eggs, separated		
¼	cup brandy		
¼	cup crème de cacao		

Sprinkle gelatin over cold water in a saucepan to soften. Blend in ⅓ cup sugar, salt and egg yolks. Cook and stir over low heat until gelatin dissolves and mixture thickens. Do not boil. Remove from heat and stir in brandy and crème de cacao. Chill until mixture starts to mound.

Beat egg whites until stiff. Gradually beat in ⅓ cup sugar. Fold whites into cooled mixture. Fold in whipped cream. Transfer filling into graham cracker crust or spoon into individual dessert dishes. Chill several hours. Garnish with chocolate curls.

8 servings

Chocolate Pecan Pie

3	eggs, beaten	1	cup chopped or halved pecans
¾	cup corn syrup	¾	cup milk chocolate chips
½	cup brown sugar	1	frozen pie crust
3	tablespoons butter, melted		
1	teaspoon vanilla		

Preheat oven to 425 degrees.

Mix together eggs, corn syrup, brown sugar, butter and vanilla. Fold in pecans and chocolate chips. Pour into frozen pie crust.

Bake 10 minutes. Reduce heat to 350 degrees and bake 20 to 30 minutes longer. Serve warm with vanilla ice cream or whipped cream.

8 servings

Blueberry Pie

¾ cup granulated sugar
¼ cup brown sugar
½ cup all-purpose flour
1 teaspoon cinnamon
½ teaspoon ground allspice
5 cups fresh blueberries

1 tablespoon lemon juice
1 tablespoon butter or margarine, melted
1 (15-ounce) package refrigerated pie crusts
1 tablespoon milk
1 teaspoon sugar

Preheat oven to 400 degrees.

Combine ¾ cup granulated sugar, brown sugar, flour, cinnamon and allspice. Add blueberries, lemon juice and butter.

Place 1 pie crust into a pie pan according to package directions. Pour blueberry filling into crust.

Roll remaining crust to ⅛-inch thickness. Cut into six 2½-inch wide or thinner strips. Arrange strips in a lattice design over filling. Fold edges under bottom crust and crimp to seal. Brush crust with milk and sprinkle with 1 teaspoon sugar.

Bake 40 to 45 minutes or until crust is golden. During last 20 minutes of baking, cover edges with foil to prevent overbrowning.

8 servings

So, my brothers, you also died to the law through the body of Christ, that you might belong to another, to him who was raised from the dead, in order that we may bear fruit to God.

~ Romans 7:4

Old Southern Pecan Pie

3 eggs, well beaten
1 cup dark corn syrup
½ cup sugar
1 cup chopped pecans

2 tablespoons butter, melted
1 teaspoon vanilla
¼ teaspoon salt
1 pie crust, unbaked

Preheat oven to 350 degrees.

Combine all ingredients except crust. Pour filling into crust. Bake 45 minutes.

8 servings

Desserts

Peggy's Krups Award Winning Sweet Potato Pie

2	(9-inch) pie crusts, unbaked	1	egg
5-6	large sweet potatoes	4	egg yolks
1	cup light brown sugar	2	teaspoons vanilla
½	cup butter or margarine	1	teaspoon lemon flavoring

Meringue

8	egg whites	½	cup sugar
1	teaspoon cream of tartar		

Preheat oven to 350 degrees.

Place pie crusts in two pie plates and prick bottoms with a fork. Place a liner of foil on top of crusts, shiny-side down, and fill with pie weights or dried beans. Bake 8 minutes. Remove weights and foil and bake 10 minutes longer. Set aside.

Boil and peel potatoes. Whip potatoes and measure out 4 cups to use in pie. Combine 4 cups hot potatoes, sugar and butter. Set aside to cool.

Using an electric mixer, beat egg and egg yolks, one at a time, into potato mixture. Beat in vanilla and lemon flavoring. Divide filling between crusts. Bake 40 minutes.

To make meringue, beat egg whites with an electric mixer on high speed until frothy. Sprinkle in cream of tartar and continue to beat until soft peaks form. Gradually beat in sugar, 1 tablespoon at a time, until stiff peaks form. Spread over baked pie and bake until meringue is lightly browned.

6 to 8 servings

Easy As Sin Chocolate Silk

1 cup butter, softened	1 teaspoon salt
½ cup cocoa powder	1 graham cracker or
4 cups powdered sugar	chocolate cookie pie
½ cup liquid pasteurized	crust or plain baked
egg	crust
¼ cup amaretto, or	Whipped cream
1 teaspoon vanilla	(optional)

Cream butter, cocoa and sugar. Beat in eggs slowly. Add amaretto and salt. Beat until smooth and shiny as silk.

Spoon into pie crust. Top with whipped cream.

8 servings

Chocolate Dream Pie

First Layer

1 cup self-rising flour	½ cup butter, softened
1 cup chopped pecans, or	
other preferred nut	

Second Layer

1 (8-ounce) package	1 cup nondairy whipped
cream cheese,	topping
softened	1 cup powdered sugar

Third Layer

2 (3-ounce) packages	3½ cups milk
instant chocolate	Whipped topping
pudding mix	

Preheat oven to 350 degrees.

Mix first layer ingredients and spread in a 9x13-inch baking dish. Bake 15 minutes. Cool.

Combine all ingredients for second layer and spread over crust.

Whip together pudding mix and milk and spoon over second layer. Refrigerate until set. Serve topped with additional whipped topping.

8 servings

My daughter Frances taught me the short-cut of using cocoa instead of baking chocolate. While she lived in New York City, her college roommate's mother, just home from surgery, wanted "one of those chocolate things your mother makes." After starting, she had no baking chocolate but lots of cocoa. We have never made it any other way since.

Chocolate Chess Pie

4	tablespoons butter	½	cup milk
1½	ounces unsweetened chocolate	2	eggs
1½	cups sugar	1	teaspoon vanilla
1	tablespoon flour	1	(9-inch) pie crust, unbaked
	Pinch of salt		

Preheat oven to 350 degrees.

Melt butter and chocolate together and pour into a mixing bowl. Add sugar, flour and salt and mix. Add milk, eggs and vanilla and beat with an electric mixer for 6 to 7 minutes.

Pour filling into pie crust. Bake 40 minutes or until firm.

8 servings

Famous Key Lime Pie

4	eggs, separated	1	(14-ounce) can sweetened condensed milk
6	tablespoons key lime juice	1	pie crust, baked

Preheat oven to 350 degrees.

Combine egg yolks, key lime juice and milk in a bowl. Mix well and pour into baked crust.

Make a meringue by beating egg whites at a high speed with an electric mixer until peaks form. Spoon onto pie. Bake 20 minutes or until meringue is browned.

8 servings

Lemon Chess Pie

A very popular Southern dessert

4	eggs	¼	cup milk
1½	cups sugar	¼	cup fresh lemon juice,
1	tablespoon flour		or ½ cup bottled
1	tablespoon cornmeal	1	(9-inch) pie crust, baked
4	tablespoons butter, melted		

Preheat oven to 325 degrees.

Beat eggs in a mixing bowl. Add sugar, flour and cornmeal. Mix in butter, milk and lemon juice.

Pour into pie crust and place a collar of foil around edge of crust. Bake 45 to 50 minutes, removing foil for last 10 minutes, or until center is firm and top is golden brown.

This is an easy pie to make, as you just mix all the ingredients in one bowl, pour into pie shell and bake.

Rector's Banana Pudding

1	(14-ounce) can Eagle Brand Condensed Milk	2	cups (1-pint) whipping cream, whipped
1½	cups cold water	40-45	vanilla wafers
1	(3.4-ounce) package instant vanilla pudding mix	4	medium bananas, sliced and dipped in lemon juice
		2	large lemons (for juice)

In mixing bowl, combine Eagle Brand Condensed Milk and water. Add pudding mix. Beat until well blended. Chill 5 minutes.

Fold in whipped cream. Spread 1 cup of pudding mixture into serving bowl.

Top with layer of vanilla wafers, then layer of bananas, then more pudding, leaving enough for two more layers. Add second and third layers (pudding, vanilla wafers, bananas), ending with remaining pudding. Chill well before serving.

8 servings

Dessert time at the Rectory usually consists of a creative combination of whatever is in the refrigerator and kitchen cabinets. The master of these random concoctions is the Rector himself! On one of these quests, Father Belser achieved his glory after combining Eagle Brand condensed milk with some overripe bananas and a forgotten box of vanilla wafers - thus producing one of our favorite desserts - the banana pudding. We all benefit when others use their gifts and talents to serve the Lord. Pass the bowls!

Desserts

213

Summer Pudding

St. Michael's steeple rises a graceful 186 feet from the ground and is topped with a gilt ball and a weather vane.

2 pounds fresh fruit, such as strawberries, blackberries, raspberries or blueberries

1 cup sugar or to taste
1 cup water
1 loaf soft white bread, crusts removed
Heavy cream

Combine fruit, sugar and water in a mixing bowl. Gently stir to mix. Simmer gently on medium heat about 20 minutes or wait until fruit softens.

Press bread slices gently against the sides of a greased deep bowl. Pour fruit into the bowl to about 2 inches deep. Add a layer of bread. Alternate layers of fruit and bread until bowl is full, ending with bread. Place a small plate upside down on top to press layers together. Place 2 cans of soda pop on top for extra weight. Refrigerate 24 hours.

To serve, invert into a serving bowl. Pour cream over the top.

Ice Cream Delight

3 cups crushed cornflakes
1 cup chopped pecans
½ cup low-fat butter, melted

1 cup brown sugar
1 cup flaked coconut
1 quart vanilla ice cream, softened
Chocolate syrup

Combine cornflakes, pecans, butter, sugar and coconut. Press ⅔ cup of mixture into a deep dish pie pan to make a crust.

Spoon ice cream into crust. Sprinkle remaining cornflake mixture on top. Freeze until ready to serve.

To serve, swirl chocolate syrup on individual serving plates. Top each plate with a slice of pie. Drizzle more syrup on top of pie.

6 to 8 servings

Desserts

Rum-Raisin Sauce

½ cup brown sugar
½ cup light corn syrup
1 tablespoon unsalted butter

¼ cup Meyers rum
¼ cup golden raisins
¼ cup dark raisins

In a small saucepan, combine sugar and corn syrup. Stir over medium heat 5 minutes or until sugar dissolves. Remove from heat. Add butter, rum and raisins. Stir until butter melts.

Serve over a premium vanilla ice cream for an impressive dessert.

This sauce is delicious over vanilla ice cream and equally as good as a sauce for ham.

Apricot Icebox Dessert

Easy

⅓ cup slivered almonds
1⅓ cups finely crushed vanilla wafer crumbs
1 teaspoon almond extract
1 tablespoon butter, melted

½ gallon vanilla ice cream
1 (12-ounce) jar apricot preserves
Whipped cream (optional)

Preheat oven to 250 to 300 degrees.

Spread almonds on a baking sheet. Toast in oven until golden; do not brown. Cool almonds and chop.

Mix chopped almonds with wafer crumbs, almond extract and butter. Spread a layer of mixture in the bottom of a lightly greased 9-inch square dish. Cut ice cream into slices and arrange in dish, completely covering the crumb mixture. Cover ice cream with a layer of preserves. Sprinkle with remaining crumb mixture. Top with whipped cream. Freeze until ready to serve.

9 or more servings

Apricot Trifle

In loving memory of my Aunt Emee Marjenhoff Anderson who liked to serve this trifle at holidays.

12	ounces apricots, dried	½	envelope unflavored
⅓	cup sugar		gelatin
18	almond macaroons,	¼	cup cool water
	crushed into crumbs	4	egg yolks
½	cup sherry	¼	cup sugar
½	cup Madeira	1	cup heavy cream
		1	teaspoon vanilla

Place apricots in a saucepan. Add enough water to cover and soak overnight. Add ⅓ cup sugar. Cook over medium heat for 1 hour. Cool and mash with a fork. Set aside.

Soak macaroon crumbs in a mixture of sherry and Madeira for at least 15 minutes. Set aside.

Sprinkle gelatin over ¼ cup cool water in a saucepan. Let stand 2 minutes, then cook and stir over low heat until thoroughly dissolved. Cool but do not allow to gel.

Place egg yolks in the top of a double boiler but not over a heat source. Whisk in ¼ cup sugar until mixture is thick and light lemon colored. Set double boiler over, but not touching, boiling water and whisk constantly over medium heat until mixture becomes thick enough to coat the back of a spoon. Whisk in dissolved gelatin. Pour mixture into a metal bowl. Set bowl in a large bowl of ice water. Whisk until mixture begins to set. Remove from ice, but do not allow mixture to set hard.

Using a chilled bowl and beaters, whip cream until soft peaks form. Add vanilla. Fold whipped cream into egg yolk mixture. If yolk mixture is too stiff, warm briefly over double boiler.

Assemble trifle in 8 to 12 compote dishes. Alternate layers of soaked macaroon crumbs, cream and apricots, ending with a dollop of cream on top of an apricot layer.

8 to 12 servings

Easy Fruit Dessert

4　pears or apples
½　cup orange juice
⅓　cup raisins

¼　cup chopped pecans
　　Dash of white wine

Place fruit in the top of a rice steamer. Add orange juice, raisins, pecans and wine. Steam until fruit is soft.

Divide fruit mixture among individual serving dishes. Serve warm topped with ice cream or your favorite topping.

4 servings

Apricot Strudel

1　cup butter or margarine
2½　cups all-purpose flour
1　cup sour cream
1　(16-ounce) jar apricot
　　jam

2　cups chopped pecans
1　(7-ounce) bag flaked
　　coconut
　　Powdered sugar

Cut butter into flour using a fork or pastry blender. Stir in sour cream. Form dough into a ball. Cover and refrigerate overnight.

When ready to bake, preheat oven to 350 degrees.

Divide dough into 3 balls. Roll each ball on a floured surface into a 12x15-inch rectangle. Spread jam over each rectangle. Sprinkle with pecans and coconut.

Roll up each jelly-roll fashion. Pinch and fold up ends. Place, seam-side down, on a greased baking sheet. Bake 1 hour or until golden brown. Cool. Cut into ¾-inch wide slices. Sprinkle with powdered sugar.

18 servings

Cranberry Ice

Great as a palette cleanser or just to be enjoyed!

Our family has used this recipe for Thanksgiving and Christmas for many generations. As we've married and multiplied, it's become a tradition for many.

4	cups cranberries		Juice of ½ lemon
4	cups water	⅔	cup cream
2	cups sugar		

Combine cranberries and water in a saucepan. Bring to a boil and cook until cranberries are soft and pop open. Strain through a colander into a saucepan, mashing mixture to squeeze through most of the cranberry pulp. Discard outer shells.

Add sugar and bring to a boil. Boil 1 minute. Cool slightly and add lemon juice. Pour into a loaf pan and freeze 2 to 3 hours or until mixture is a soft mush. Stir in cream. Cover and freeze until ready to serve.

10 to 12 servings

Seven Layer Sour Cream Torte

3	cups sifted flour	2	cups chopped walnuts
1½	cups sugar	1½	cups powdered sugar
1	cup butter, softened	1	pint sour cream
1	egg	1	teaspoon vanilla

Mix flour and sugar. Blend in butter. Stir in egg and mix with hands until dough holds together. If needed, add more flour. Divide dough into 7 balls and chill.

Preheat oven to 350 degrees.

Roll out dough into seven 9-inch circles and place each in a pie pan or on a baking sheet. Bake 10 to 12 minutes or until edges brown. Cool.

Mix walnuts, powdered sugar, sour cream and vanilla. Stack cookie layers, spreading sour cream mixture between layers. Sprinkle extra powdered sugar on top.

Chill at least 5 hours. Cut into thin slices to serve.

12 to 14 servings

Two 18-ounce cans of refrigerated sugar cookie dough can be used. Divide into 7 parts and proceed as directed above.

Desserts

Strawberries Brûlée

1	(8-ounce) package cream cheese, softened	2	pints strawberries, hulled, sliced and sweetened to taste
1½	cups sour cream	1	cup brown sugar
6	tablespoons granulated sugar		

Beat cream cheese in a mixing bowl until fluffy. Add sour cream and granulated sugar and blend thoroughly.

Arrange strawberries in a shallow ovenproof serving dish. Spoon cream mixture over top. Sprinkle with brown sugar.

Place dish on lowest broiler rack. Broil until sugar bubbles and browns lightly. Serve immediately.

6 to 8 servings

Bavarian Torte

Crust

½	cup butter or margarine, melted	¾	cup pecan meal or finely chopped pecans
¼	cup sugar	½	teaspoon salt
¼	cup flour	1	teaspoon vanilla

Filling

1	(8-ounce) package cream cheese (regular or low-fat)	1	egg
		⅓	cup sugar
		1	teaspoon vanilla

Topping

1	pear, sliced	1	teaspoon cinnamon
½	cup sugar		

Preheat oven to 400 degrees.

Combine all crust ingredients and mix well. Press mixture into the bottom and up the sides of a 7-inch springform pan.

Beat together all filling ingredients and pour over crust.

For topping, arrange pear slices over filling. Mix together sugar and cinnamon and sprinkle on top. Bake 40 to 45 minutes.

6 to 8 servings

Caramel Icing

Excellent served on yellow cake

½ cup margarine or butter
1 cup brown sugar
¼ cup milk

½ teaspoon vanilla
2 cups powdered sugar, sifted
Pinch of salt

Melt margarine with brown sugar slowly in a saucepan. When mixture begins to boil, cook and stir 2 minutes. Add milk and bring to a boil, stirring constantly. Remove from heat and cool 10 minutes.

Add vanilla, powdered sugar and salt. Beat until smooth and thick enough to spread without running off cake.

Pastel Melt-Aways

I made these for a bridal shower and the pleading for more hasn't stopped yet!

Cookie

¾ cup margarine or butter, softened
½ cup powdered sugar

½ cup cornstarch
1 cup all-purpose flour

Icing

1½ cups powdered sugar
1 teaspoon vanilla
1 tablespoon margarine or butter, softened

2-3 tablespoons milk
Food coloring

Preheat oven to 325 degrees.

Combine margarine and sugar in a large bowl. Blend thoroughly. Stir in cornstarch and flour. If needed, chill dough 30 minutes for easier handling.

Shape dough into ¾-inch balls and place 2 inches apart on an ungreased baking sheet. Bake 10 to 13 minutes or until lightly browned around the edges. Cool completely.

In a small bowl, combine all icing ingredients except food coloring. If necessary, add a few more drops of milk to reach desired consistency. Divide icing into several small bowls. Tint each bowl as desired with different food colorings. Spoon icing over cookies.

42 servings

Meringues

4 egg whites	1 cup miniature chocolate chips (optional)
1 teaspoon cream of tartar	1 cup slivered almonds (optional)
1 cup sugar	
1 teaspoon vanilla	
1 cup chopped pecans (optional)	

Preheat oven to 275 degrees.

Beat egg whites with cream of tartar until soft peaks form. Gradually add sugar, beating constantly. Fold in vanilla. Add pecans, chocolate chips or almonds, if desired.

Drop by spoonfuls onto a parchment paper-lined baking sheet. Bake 25 minutes. Turn off heat and leave in oven until completely cooled; overnight is best. Do not open oven door until cooled. Store in an airtight container.

About 36 cookies

"For my flesh is real food and my blood real drink. Whoever eats my flesh and drinks my blood remains in me and I in him."

~ John 6:55-56

Swedish Butter Creams

1 cup butter, softened	2 cups sifted flour
⅓ cup heavy cream	Granulated sugar

Buttercream Frosting

4 tablespoons butter, softened	1 teaspoon vanilla
1 cup powdered sugar	Food coloring
1 egg yolk	Colored sugar

Preheat oven to 375 degrees.

Cream butter until light and fluffy. Gradually beat in cream. Gradually mix in flour. Chill dough several hours in plastic wrap.

On a lightly floured surface, roll dough to ⅛-inch thickness. Use a 1½-inch cookie cutter to cut out cookies. Dip each side of cookie into sugar and prick with a fork. Bake 7 to 8 minutes. Cool on a rack.

To make frosting, cream butter, powdered sugar, egg yolk and vanilla. Tint as desired with food coloring. Spread frosting over cookies and sprinkle with colored sugar.

Color these with red and green frosting and enjoy as Christmas cookies.

Desserts

Custard

From my grandmother, Ferdinand Williams Alexander. Men love this, particularly when they are sick.

3 eggs	1 cup milk
¼ cup sugar	1 cup half-and-half
1 teaspoon vanilla	

Preheat oven to 325 degrees.

Beat eggs. Mix in sugar and vanilla. Meanwhile, heat milk and half-and-half in a saucepan. When hot, but not quite boiling, add to egg mixture and stir.

Pour mixture into custard cups. Place cups in a pan of water and bake 30 to 45 minutes or until a knife inserted in the custard comes out clean.

Miss Rachel's F.H.A. Chocolate Oatmeal Cookies

My best friends and I would always make these cookies during slumber parties. They're easy, quick and delicious with a glass of cold milk.

2 cups sugar	½ cup cocoa powder
½ cup butter	1 teaspoon vanilla
½ cup milk	½ cup peanut butter
2 cups dry quick-cooking oats	

Combine sugar, butter and milk in a saucepan. Bring to a boil over medium heat. Boil 2 to 3 minutes. Remove from heat.

Stir in oats, cocoa, vanilla and peanut butter. Beat with a spoon until mixture begins to thicken. Drop by spoonfuls onto wax paper or foil and cool.

32 cookies

Desserts

Brownies

¾	cup butter	3	cups sugar
4	(1-ounce) squares unsweetened chocolate	2	cups flour
		1	teaspoon salt
		2	teaspoons vanilla
6	eggs	1	cup chopped pecans

Frosting

½	cup butter, softened	1	teaspoon salt
2-3	cups powdered sugar	1	teaspoon vanilla
½	cup cocoa		Cream

Preheat oven to 425 degrees.

Melt butter and chocolate together in the microwave on low to medium power.

In a mixing bowl, beat eggs until fluffy. Add sugar and beat well. Beat in melted chocolate mixture. Add flour, salt, vanilla and pecans, beating well after each addition. Pour batter into a greased 9x13-inch baking pan. Bake 30 minutes. Cool.

To make frosting, cream butter, sugar and cocoa. Add salt and vanilla. Slowly add enough cream to make frosting spreadable. Spread over cooled brownies.

I've made these since the 1940's. Once I tried a different recipe and my son asked what was wrong with the brownies. I said, "I used a different recipe." His reply was, "You WHAT?!"

Oatmeal-Rice Crispie Cookies

1	cup butter	2	cups flour
1	cup granulated sugar	1	teaspoon baking soda
1	cup brown sugar	½	teaspoon salt
2	eggs, beaten	2	cups dry oatmeal
1	teaspoon orange or vanilla extract	2	cups crisp rice cereal
1	tablespoon orange zest		Chopped nuts (optional)

Cream butter and sugars. Add eggs, extract and zest.

Sift flour, baking soda and salt together and add to creamed mixture. Mix in oatmeal. Stir in cereal and nuts. Refrigerate at least 1 hour or until firm.

When ready to bake, preheat oven to 375 degrees.

Drop dough by teaspoonfuls onto a greased baking sheet. Bake 10 to 12 minutes. Cool on a wire rack.

8 dozen

Desserts

Sands

At Christmas, I
make 2 batches,
putting red food
coloring in one and
green in the other
- very festive!

1	cup butter	2	cups sifted flour
¼	cup powdered sugar	1	cup finely chopped
2	teaspoons vanilla		pecans
1	tablespoon water		Powdered sugar

Preheat oven to 300 degrees.

Cream butter and ¼ cup powdered sugar. Add vanilla and water. Blend in flour and pecans. Roll into bite-size balls and place on an ungreased baking sheet.

Bake 20 minutes or until delicately browned on the bottom. Roll immediately in powdered sugar, rolling twice in sugar if needed.

5 to 5½ dozen

The Best
Chocolate Chip Cookies

While on
the testing
committee
I had the
pleasure of
testing this
recipe. It was so
good I tested it
over 10 times!
The cookbook
committee
chairman, after
noticing the
recipe missing for
a while, strongly
suggested I make
a copy of the
recipe for myself
and return the
original so that
others may enjoy
it too.

½	cup butter	1	teaspoon baking soda
½	cup vegetable	1	teaspoon salt
	shortening	1	cup chopped pecans or
1	cup brown sugar		walnuts, toasted
½	cup granulated sugar	1	(12-ounce) package
2	eggs, beaten		semi-sweet chocolate
2½	cups unsifted flour		chips (2 cups)

Preheat oven to 350 degrees.

Cream butter, shortening and sugars together. Beat in eggs. Blend in flour, baking soda and salt. Stir in toasted nuts and chocolate chips. Drop by spoonfuls onto a greased baking sheet.

Bake 8 to 10 minutes in the top half of the oven.

35 to 40 cookies

Desserts

Mama's Oatmeal Cookies

Great paired with ice cream!

2	cups flour	1	cup brown sugar
1	teaspoon baking soda	2	eggs
½	teaspoon salt	¼	cup sherry
2	teaspoons cinnamon	4	cups dry quick oats
½	teaspoon nutmeg	1	cup raisins
1	cup margarine	½	cup chopped pecans
1	cup granulated sugar		(optional)

Preheat oven to 350 degrees.

Stir together flour, baking soda, salt, cinnamon and nutmeg.

In a separate bowl, cream margarine. Beat in sugars. Mix in eggs. Add half of the dry ingredients and stir until mixed. Stir in sherry. Mix in remainder of dry ingredients. Add oats, raisins and pecans. Drop by teaspoonfuls about 2 inches apart onto a greased baking sheet.

Bake 10 to 12 minutes. Remove from baking sheet and cool on a wire rack.

About 5 dozen

I remember making these oatmeal cookies with my mother when I was about 10 years old.

Yummy Joes

2	cups flour	1	egg, separated
1	cup sugar	2	teaspoons vanilla
½	cup margarine, softened	¼	teaspoon salt
½	cup butter, softened	½	cup chopped nuts

Preheat oven to 250 degrees.

Combine flour, sugar, margarine, butter, egg yolk, vanilla and salt. Beat until light. Spread dough on a jelly roll pan. Beat egg white and brush lightly over dough. Sprinkle with nuts.

Bake 45 to 60 minutes. Remove from oven and cut immediately into squares. Cool in pan.

Confetti Shortbread Stars

Cookies

2	cups flour	1	cup butter
½	cup superfine sugar	3	tablespoons orange zest
3	hard-cooked egg yolks, rubbed through a sieve		Pinch of salt

Orange Glaze

1½	cups powdered sugar	Yellow food coloring
½	teaspoon orange zest	Decorating sprinkles
1½-2	tablespoons orange juice	

Preheat oven to 400 degrees.

Blend together all cookie ingredients. Knead dough and divide into fourths. Chill dough 3 hours.

Working with a quarter of dough at a time, roll out to ⅛- to ¼-inch thick. Cut out cookies with a star-shaped cookie cutter. Bake 7 to 8 minutes. Cool.

To make glaze, mix sugar, zest and orange juice until smooth and thick. Tint with food coloring. Spoon icing over cookies, covering them completely. Decorate with sprinkles. Let stand until glaze sets.

Blitz Kuchen Recipe

"Fine old recipe"

1	cup butter, softened	1½	cups flour
4	eggs		Chopped almonds or pecans
1	cup sugar		Cinnamon sugar
	Zest of 1 lemon		

Preheat oven to 350 degrees.

Cream butter. Beat in eggs, one at a time. Add sugar and lemon zest. Mix in flour. Spread dough into a very thin layer on a greased baking sheet.

Sprinkle with nuts and gently press them in. Sprinkle with cinnamon sugar. Bake until done. Cut into small squares while still warm.

164 squares

Desserts

Ranger Cookies

1	cup margarine	½	teaspoon salt
1	cup granulated sugar	2	cups dry oats
1	cup brown sugar	1	cup coconut
2	eggs, beaten	2	cup wheat flakes cereal
2	cups flour	1½	teaspoons vanilla
1	teaspoon baking soda	1	teaspoon almond
1	teaspoon baking powder		extract

Preheat oven to 350 degrees.

Cream margarine and sugars. Mix in eggs. Sift together flour, baking soda, baking powder and salt and blend into creamed mixture. Add oats, coconut, cereal, vanilla and almond extract. Mix well.

Drop by teaspoonfuls onto a foil-lined baking sheet. Bake about 12 minutes.

During its existence, St. Michael's has been useful to the entire community. As early as 1762, the fire engine was kept in its yard, and as late as 1821 fire buckets were kept there.

Lacy Benne Wafers

1	cup benne seeds (sesame seeds), toasted	1	cup light brown sugar
		1	teaspoon vanilla
¾	cup plus 1 tablespoon butter	1	egg
		¼	teaspoon baking powder
¾	cup flour	¼	teaspoon salt

Preheat oven to 400 degrees.

To toast benne seeds, sprinkle seeds on a baking sheet sprayed with nonstick cooking spray. Toast 10 minutes, shaking pan occasionally while baking. Watch very carefully to prevent burning.

Mix toasted seeds with all remaining ingredients by hand or with an electric mixer. Drop by small teaspoonfuls onto a foil-lined baking sheet. Bake at 375 degrees for 6 minutes or until light brown. Remove from foil when cooled. Store in an airtight container.

Desserts

Momma's Healthy Treat

A great healthy treat

1 cup peanut butter	1 cup raisins or chopped
½ cup honey	dried fruit
1 cup dry old-fashioned	½ cup wheat germ
oats	1 cup coconut

Combine all ingredients except coconut. Shape dough into 1-inch balls. Roll balls in coconut.

35 to 37 balls

Hermits

3 cups flour	¾ cup butter or margarine,
½ teaspoon salt	softened
1 teaspoon baking	⅔ cup granulated sugar
powder	¾ cup brown sugar
1 teaspoon cinnamon	2 eggs, beaten
1 teaspoon ground cloves	1 cup raisins
1 teaspoon ground ginger	1 cup chopped walnuts
¼ cup molasses	1 egg, beaten
2 tablespoons warm	
water	

Preheat oven to 350 degrees.

Combine flour, salt, baking powder, cinnamon, cloves and ginger. Set aside. In a small bowl, mix molasses with warm water.

In a large mixing bowl, cream butter and sugars. Beat in 2 eggs. Add dry ingredients and molasses. Mix well. Fold in raisins and walnuts.

Spread the batter in 2 rows on each of 2 greased baking sheets, shaping the rows with a spatula into strips about 10 inches long and 3 inches wide. Space rows several inches apart. Brush the top of each row with beaten egg.

Bake 15 minutes or to desired degree of crispness. Cut each strip into 9 bars while still warm. Serve with applesauce.

36 bars

Mystery Cookies

½ cup margarine, melted
1½ cups graham cracker crumbs
1 (6-ounce) package chocolate chips
1 (6-ounce) package butterscotch chips

1 (14-ounce) can sweetened condensed milk
1 cup coconut
1 cup pecans

This is a super easy recipe and very quick to make - it's as good as it is easy.

Preheat oven to 350 degrees.

Mix margarine and cracker crumbs. Press into the bottom of a 9x13-inch baking pan. Sprinkle with chocolate chips and butterscotch chips. Pour milk over chips. Sprinkle with coconut and pecans.

Bake 30 minutes. Cool and cut into squares.

24 to 36 servings

Peanut Butter Sticks

Very tasty

1 (16-ounce) jar peanut butter

3 tablespoons vegetable oil
1 loaf day-old bread

Blend peanut butter and oil until creamy. Trim and save crust from bread. Cut each bread slice into 4 strips. Toast trimmed crust and bread strips until lightly browned. Roll bread strips in creamed mixture and set aside.

Crush toasted crust into crumbs. Roll peanut butter-coated strips in crumbs until covered. Place on paper towels for 1 hour. Store in an airtight container and keep cool.

5 to 6 dozen

Desserts

The Best Gingersnaps Ever

When adding sticky ingredients such as molasses or honey, first spray the measuring cup with nonstick cooking spray. All of the molasses will end up in the recipe insuring precise measurement. As a bonus, the measuring cup is much easier to clean.

¾ cup vegetable shortening
1 cup sugar
1 egg
¼ cup molasses
2 cups all-purpose unbleached flour
½ teaspoon salt
2 teaspoons baking soda
1 heaping teaspoon cinnamon
¾ teaspoon ground cloves
¾ teaspoon ground ginger
Pinch of nutmeg
Sugar for rolling cookies

Cream shortening and sugar in a mixing bowl using an electric mixer. Add egg and molasses and beat until blended, scraping sides of bowl as needed.

In a separate bowl, combine flour, salt, baking soda, cinnamon, cloves, ginger and nutmeg. Mix thoroughly. Add dry ingredients, about 1 cup at a time, to creamed mixture, scraping sides down after each addition. Gather dough into a ball and flatten into a large disk. Wrap in plastic and refrigerate 2 hours.

When ready to bake, preheat oven to 400 degrees.

Roll dough into 2-inch balls. Roll balls in sugar and place on an ungreased baking sheet. Flatten slightly with the bottom of a glass. Bake 12 to 14 minutes. Cool slightly on baking sheet before removing to a wire rack to cool completely.

About 3 dozen

Bourbon Balls

2 cups chopped pecans
Bourbon
1 cup butter, melted
2 pounds powdered sugar
8 (1-ounce) squares semi-sweet chocolate
¼ bar paraffin wax

Soak pecans in bourbon for 2 weeks. Drain. Mix melted butter and powdered sugar with pecans. Shape into balls. Freeze 15 minutes.

Meanwhile, melt chocolate and wax together. Dip balls into chocolate mixture. Place on wax paper to cool.

Lemon Squares

2	cups flour, sifted	¼	cup lemon juice
½	cup powdered sugar	4	eggs, slightly beaten
1	cup butter, softened		Zest of 1 lemon
½	teaspoon salt		Powdered sugar for
2	cups granulated sugar		topping

Preheat oven to 350 degrees.

Knead flour, powdered sugar, butter and salt together. Press into the bottom of an ungreased 9x13-inch baking pan. Bake 4 minutes.

Mix granulated sugar, lemon juice, eggs and zest together. Pour mixture over baked crust. Bake 25 minutes at 325 degrees. Sprinkle with powdered sugar while still warm. Cool before cutting.

24 servings

Shortbread Squares

2	cups butter or margarine, softened	2	egg yolks
1½	cups sugar	5	cups unsifted all-purpose flour

Preheat oven to 325 degrees.

Cream butter in a mixing bowl until soft and smooth. Gradually beat in sugar until light and fluffy. Beat in egg yolks. Gradually blend in flour until well mixed. Knead dough in bowl for 1 minute.

Divide into quarters. Press each quarter into a 9x13-inch baking pan. Dough should be ¼-inch thick. Cut each pan of dough into 24 squares and prick with a fork. Bake 20 to 30 minutes; shortbread should be pale yellow and not allowed to brown. Cut while hot. Cool.

8 dozen

Aunt Ethel's Heavenly Fudge

Great gift for neighbors and teachers at Christmas.

4 cups sugar	1 (12-ounce) package semi- sweet chocolate chips
¾ cup butter	
1 (12-ounce) can evaporated milk	25 large marshmallows
	1½ teaspoons vanilla
	1 cup pecans (optional)

Cook sugar, butter and milk in a saucepan over medium heat to soft-ball stage (234 to 240 degrees on a candy thermometer). Immediately remove from heat and add in chocolate chips, marshmallows, vanilla and nuts. Stir until well mixed. Pour mixture into a 9x13-inch dish. Cool until set.

4 pounds

Peanut Butter Fudge

½ cup butter, melted	1 tablespoon vanilla
1 cup peanut butter	2 cups powdered sugar

Mix butter, peanut butter and vanilla. Add sugar. Refrigerate 1 hour or freeze.

For chocolate fudge, use 1 cup chocolate chips instead of peanut butter.

Chewy Chip Bars

¾ cup butter, softened	½ teaspoon baking powder
1¾ cup sugar	
2 eggs	3 cups raisin bran cereal
1 teaspoon vanilla	1 (12-ounce) package chocolate chips
1 cup flour	
½ teaspoon salt	

Preheat oven to 350 degrees.

Cream butter and sugar. Mix in eggs and vanilla. Add flour, salt, baking powder and cereal. Mix well.

Spread mixture in a greased 9x13-inch baking pan. Cover with chocolate chips. Bake 30 minutes.

Desserts

Apricot Squares

1	cup butter, softened	¾	cup walnuts
1	cup sugar	1	(10-ounce) jar apricot
1	egg yolk		jam
2	cups all-purpose flour		

Preheat oven to 350 degrees.

Cream butter and sugar in a large bowl. Add egg yolk and mix well. Stir in flour. Add walnuts and blend.

Divide dough in half. Spread first half evenly over the bottom of a 9x13-inch baking pan. Cover with jam. Drop remaining dough by spoonfuls over jam, spreading carefully with the edge of a knife.

Bake 40 to 45 minutes or until top is golden. Cool slightly before cutting.

35 (½-inch) squares

Date Squares

1¼	pounds dates	1	cup brown sugar
1	cup water	1	teaspoon baking soda
	Scant ¼ cup granulated sugar	1½	cups flour
1	tablespoon flour	1	cup margarine
2	cups dry oatmeal or more if needed		Dash of salt

Preheat oven to 350 degrees.

Combine dates, water, granulated sugar and 1 tablespoon flour in a saucepan. Bring to a boil. Cook and stir until thickened. Set aside.

Mix oatmeal, brown sugar, baking soda, 1½ cups flour, margarine and salt. Press about three-fourths of dough onto a baking sheet. Spread date mixture on top. Sprinkle with remaining dough, adding more oatmeal to dough if needed.

Bake 40 to 45 minutes. Cut into squares.

Lib's Blond Brownies

Unusual epitaphs in the graveyard:

"View this tomb as you pass by, For as you are so once was I, And as I am, so must you be; Prepare yourself to follow me."

"The beautiful she have faded from our track, We mourn her but we cannot bring her back."

And over the grave of a sea Captain is the nautical stanza,

"Although I here at anchor be With many of our fleet, We must set sail one day again Our Savior Christ to meet."

Another tells of the mother of nine children, who died, "age 17 years and 27 days."

¾	cup margarine	2¼	teaspoons baking powder
1	(16-ounce) box light brown sugar	1	teaspoon salt
3	eggs, beaten		Nuts
1	teaspoon vanilla	½	(12-ounce) package semi-sweet chocolate chips
2¼	cups flour		

Preheat oven to 350 degrees.

Melt margarine and sugar in a saucepan. Stir well and set aside to cool. Add eggs to butter mixture. Stir in vanilla.

Sift together flour, baking powder and salt. Add dry ingredients to butter mixture. Mix well; dough will be stiff. Stir in nuts. Spread evenly in a 9x13-inch baking pan. Sprinkle chocolate chips on top. Bake 20 to 30 minutes or until done.

Iren Marik's London Slices

2	cups flour	5-6	egg whites
10	tablespoons butter	2	cups powdered sugar
½	cup powdered sugar	2	cups finely grated walnuts or pecans
2	egg yolks		
	Raspberry jam		

Preheat oven to 350 degrees.

Mix together flour, butter, ½ cup powdered sugar and egg yolks. Press into a baking pan. Cover with jam.

Beat egg whites until stiff. Mix in 2 cups powdered sugar. Fold in nuts. Pour mixture over jam. Bake 50 minutes.

Desserts

234

$\mathscr{A}$

$\mathscr{B}$

C

CAULIFLOWER

CEREALS & GRAINS
(also see Grits and Rice)

CHEESE

E

F

G

M

MELONS

MUSHROOMS

N

NUTS

O

OKRA

ONIONS

OYSTER *(see Seafood)*

P

S

SALAD DRESSINGS

SALADS

SANDWICHES

SAUCES *(see Condiments & Sauces)*

SEAFOOD

V

W

Art from St. Michael's Cookbook

P.O. Box 832
Charleston, South Carolina 29401

Name: _____

Address: _____

City: _____ State: _____ Zip: _____

Telephone: _____

Order Form

Name of Print(s)	Print Size	Frame? (yes/no)	Cost

Sub-Total	
6% Sales Tax	
Shipping Cost	
Total	

**Make check payable to
St. Michael's Cookbook**

Size of Prints	Print Cost		Shipping	Shipping
	W/O Frame	With Frame	W/O Frame	With Frame
Full: Limited Edition of 50, Signed by Artist, 24¾ x 17½	$400.00	$500.00	$12.00	$25.00
Half: Unlimited	$100.00	$160.00	$12.00	$25.00
Small: Unlimited	$25.00	$55.00	$12.00	$25.00

*The prices shown above for prints, frames, taxes, and shipping are
subject to possible adjustment after December 31, 2002.*

Cookbook Location		Name of Print(s)
	Cover	St. Michael's Church
	Divider	Ruthie's Dog
	Divider	St. Michael's at Sunrise
	Divider	Mid-Day Prayer
	Divider	St. Michael's Bell Ringers
	Divider	St. Michael's Altar at Christmas
	Divider	Baptism
	Divider	Cross at Kanuga
	Divider	Easter Egg Hunt

Faithfully Charleston

250 years of Meals and Memories
P.O. Box 832
Charleston, South Carolina 29401

Name: _____

Address: _____

City: _____ State: _____ Zip: _____

Please make all checks payable to St. Michael's Cookbook.

If you wish to order 1 to 5 cookbooks, use this section of the form.

Please send _____ copy(ies)	@ $19.95 each	
Postage and Handling	@ $ 3.95 each	
	Total	

If you wish to order 6 or more cookbooks, use this section of the form.

Please send _____ copies	@ $18.95 each	
Postage and Handling	@ $ 3.95 each	
	Total	

The prices shown above for cookbooks, postage and handling,
and sales tax are subject to possible adjustment after December 31, 2002.

- -

Faithfully Charleston

250 years of Meals and Memories
P.O. Box 832
Charleston, South Carolina 29401

Name: _____

Address: _____

City: _____ State: _____ Zip: _____

Please make all checks payable to St. Michael's Cookbook.

If you wish to order 1 to 5 cookbooks, use this section of the form.

Please send _____ copy(ies)	@ $19.95 each	
Postage and Handling	@ $ 3.95 each	
	Total	

If you wish to order 6 or more cookbooks, use this section of the form.

Please send _____ copies	@ $18.95 each	
Postage and Handling	@ $ 3.95 each	
	Total	

The prices shown above for cookbooks, postage and handling,
and sales tax are subject to possible adjustment after December 31, 2002.

Faithfully Charleston

250 years of Meals and Memories
P.O. Box 832
Charleston, South Carolina 29401

Name: _____

Address: _____

City: _____ State: _____ Zip: _____

Please make all checks payable to St. Michael's Cookbook.

If you wish to order 1 to 5 cookbooks, use this section of the form.

Please send _____ copy(ies)	@ $19.95 each	
Postage and Handling	@ $ 3.95 each	
	Total	

If you wish to order 6 or more cookbooks, use this section of the form.

Please send _____ copies	@ $18.95 each	
Postage and Handling	@ $ 3.95 each	
	Total	

The prices shown above for cookbooks, postage and handling,
and sales tax are subject to possible adjustment after December 31, 2002.

- -

Faithfully Charleston

250 years of Meals and Memories
P.O. Box 832
Charleston, South Carolina 29401

Name: _____

Address: _____

City: _____ State: _____ Zip: _____

Please make all checks payable to St. Michael's Cookbook.

If you wish to order 1 to 5 cookbooks, use this section of the form.

Please send _____ copy(ies)	@ $19.95 each	
Postage and Handling	@ $ 3.95 each	
	Total	

If you wish to order 6 or more cookbooks, use this section of the form.

Please send _____ copies	@ $18.95 each	
Postage and Handling	@ $ 3.95 each	
	Total	

The prices shown above for cookbooks, postage and handling,
and sales tax are subject to possible adjustment after December 31, 2002.